SOUTHERN WOMEN

Their Wisdom, Wit and Wickedness!

Tips. Traditions. Insights. How-To's.
Favorite Southern Recipes. Road Trips!

By Sylvia Higginbotham

Copyright © 2004 by Sylvia Higginbotham

All rights reserved.

No part of this book may be reproduced or transmitted in any form, except for reviews, without the written permission of the publisher.

PARLANCE PUBLISHING
P.O. Box 841
Columbus, Mississippi 39703

Printed in Birmingham, Alabama
By EBSCO Media

ISBN 0-9721032-3-6

Library of Congress Control Number
2004096008

Cover Art: "Southern Friends" by native Mississippi artist Eugenia Talbott, Medford, Oregon

SOUTHERN WOMEN

Their Wisdom, Wit, and Wickedness!

By Sylvia Higginbotham

Chapter 1 — Page 1
The Little Foxes (Lillian Hellman)
    From Girl to Southern Woman (Tips: on being a Southern woman)

Chapter 2 — Page 13
A Good Man is Hard to Find (Flannery O'Connor)
    Meeting, Dating, Mating (Tips: where, when, how)

Chapter 3 — Page 21
A Member of the Wedding (Carson McCullers)
    Men, Marriage, Sex (Tips: wedding how-tos, marital bliss)

Chapter 4 — Page 30
Rocking Chair Blues (Bessie Smith)
    Birthing Babies

Chapter 5 — Page 36
Making a Mark (Mary McCloud Bethune)
    Confidence and Charisma

Chapter 6 **One of Ours** (Willa Cather) Notable and Well-known Southern Women	Page 42
Chapter 7 **The Worn Path** (Eudora Welty) Old Southern Remedies that Work Today	Page 50
Chapter 8 **Career-wise and Otherwise** (The Grimke Sisters) Woman's Work is Never Done	Page 60
Chapter 9 **The World I Live In** (Helen Keller) Words of Wisdom	Page 68
Chapter 10 **Fabulous Southern Food!** Ageless Favorite Recipes and Road Trips!	Page 83

INTRODUCTION

Southern women know things. They are expert at "making do" when necessary and "coming through" when called upon. They're book smart, street smart, and just plain savvy. They can deliver a powerful business presentation that makes everyone present sit up and take notice. They can plan, implement and present a perfect sit-down dinner party for 24, yet they're just as adept at serving up superb comfort food for a few close friends who appreciate a soul food supper. Indeed, they are hospitable, gracious, friendly and kind. Southern women — even with a few foibles, faults and perhaps an occasional wicked streak — are the best of the best.

The art of being a Southern woman is a birth right for any baby girl born south of the Mason-Dixon line. It's an art form passed down from great grandmothers, grandmothers, mothers, godmothers, and aunts. And those not fortunate enough to be born Southern but still want the honor of being a Southern woman can always marry a Southern man. Many a transplanted Yankee wife practices "Southernese" like a pro, but it's never quite the same. They join the Southern sisterhood, but they seldom progress past the status of stepsisters.

There are many varieties of Southern women, and we'll touch upon many of them in this book as we look at the ways in which they're special. We'll look at the outrageousness that keeps us talking, the humor that keeps us laughing, and the wisdom that is inherited from our foremothers and implemented by the distinguished Southern women who make us all look good. We'll also get a glimpse of the wayward ways that come to the surface on occasion. A modicum of wickedness every now and then is acceptable for it keeps things from getting boring, though "tacky" is a dreaded word. Southern women do not take kindly to being called "tacky." It's a word right up there with "low rent," another phrase that is anathema to the sisterhood.

There's no place I'd rather be than at a girlfriend reunion at an old fishing camp on a lake or a mountain lodge down South! If the reunion occurs in a glamorous and glitzy place, there are too many distractions and the Southern sisters don't want to miss a thing. To get the full effect, it's more fun in the quiet zone. Whenever the girls, or perhaps the not so genteel older women get together to reminisce, good times are sure to follow.

People outside the South may not be aware of the fact that Southern women are accomplished in most every field. We believe that behind every good man is a great woman – either mother or wife. Therefore, we thought it would be appropriate to call attention to the literary and leadership prowess of Southern women. You will note that we used some of them to set up the chapters and that gave us an opportunity to talk about a few of their accomplishments.

Thanks to Southern women, this book is full of expert advice from friends who are attorneys, judges, ministers, teachers, interior designers, artists, medical professionals, entrepreneurs, bankers, happily marrieds, divorcees, daughters, grandmothers, and great grandmothers. Thank you all for your interest, suggestions, answers to questions, and encouragement! Though I am at least a sixth generation Southern woman and have been an apt pupil and observer of the damsels of Dixie for more years than I care to admit, this book is the result of family ties, friendships, relationships, and years of research and serious note-taking.

From talents to tantrums (called hissy-fits down South), we hope that our favorite Southern women will continue to do their part to make life interesting. After all, there are traditions to be upheld, and tradition still maintains a place of honor in the South.

This one is for you, Mother.

FLOYE TEMPLE ROBBINS, 1914-1998.

CHAPTER 1
The Little Foxes
Lillian Hellman

Lillian Hellman, one of America's few successful female playwrights, was born in New Orleans in 1905 and was Southern by birth and spirit. She was considered "plain" in appearance, but her talent, energy, courage and confidence were most attractive to the men in her life, and there were many. Perhaps the relationship best known was with fellow writer, the dashing Dashiell Hammett, who was totally enamored of his "Lily."

Her plays were known for their creation of tragedy and conflict, with many of them set in the South. She wrote *The Little Foxes* in 1939, which emphasized material greed and lust for power. Other well-known works were *The Children's Hour* and *Toys in the Attic.* Hellman's *Scoundrel Time* recounted Congressional investigations of Communist influence in the U.S. during what has been called Joseph McCarthy's Communist witch-hunt. Many Hollywood careers were ruined during this time.

Hellman was cited for her courageous defiance of the House Committee on Un-American Activities in 1952, an act that almost landed her in jail. She remained concerned with social issues all her life. Ms. Hellman lived and worked in Martha's Vineyard in summer and New York City in winter, though she kept her strong ties to the South.

She started writing books instead of plays in 1960, when a reviewer said that the three greatest living American playwrights were Edward Albee, Tennessee Williams, and Arthur Miller. Hellman was the subject of five books. She led an active and creative life, though when she died in 1984 at the age of 79, she was crippled, legally blind and weighed 80 pounds.

From Little Girl to Southern Woman

The lyrics of an old song come to mind: "Thank heaven for little girls, for little girls get bigger every day." There comes a time, much too soon for the parents, that these darling little girls emerge into stone foxes, thus they are "the little foxes." Personalities form at an early age, and it's yet to be determined if social behavior is the result of genetics or if "it's all in the raisin'" as my dear mother often said.

Whichever theory applies, almost from the time they're toddlers, it's easy to see which personality type will best suit the Southern girl. To offer a better look at differences, we've placed the girls/women in categories based on their upbringing and actions. You'll recognize them throughout this book, for they are wise, worldly, and sometimes wild women. They make a place for themselves wherever they go. We hope they never lose those unique qualities that get better with age and insight. Now, let's meet our Miss Precious.

"Whatever happens in life is either a blessing or a lesson."

Miss Precious/Mrs. Perfect

Precious is Daddy's Darlin' who more than likely grew up on a big farm, once called a plantation, in the middle of thousands of acres of flat, rich land. Precious is what we know as "spoiled" and perhaps a bit on the selfish side. Later, you'll find her at boarding schools and certain colleges where she always breaks the rules or makes new ones, all the while acting as though she would never do anything wrong. How could anyone suggest such a thing! Daddy would be furious!

Precious is trained to marry well, and so she does. Once she's way past her college years, she's still back on campus, because college was indeed her glory time and she never quite got past it. You'll see her at tailgate parties, class reunions, or serving on some alumni committee that requires her presence on campus. Precious is hard to miss because she is always dressed to the nines with perfectly colored and coiffed hair, a lovely tan, and the best teeth, wrinkle-free skin and porcelain nails that money can buy. Precious would be right at home at Ole Miss, the school that produced more "Miss Americas" than any other, among them Mary Ann Mobley, now an actress, Lynda Lee Mead, and Susan Aiken.

Don't cross Precious, even when Daddy's long gone and she's up in years herself, because she is accustomed to getting her way. Nothing is too good for our girl Precious. If anyone dares to deny her, a hissy-fit is to be expected. And in her case, a hissy fit can spawn meanness if she's a Precious who has that tendency. Such tactics may be cute in an adorable little girl, but as a grown woman, it can be less than attractive. Precious is generally not the Southern woman who inspires love and adoration in anyone but dear old Daddy. Does she sound like Helen Reddy's song, "Delta Dawn"? We all know one or two Preciouses, and wouldn't we love to shake them! But there again, Precious is one of the Southern women who add to the mystique, and deep down, she's kind-hearted and even generous to her family and a few good friends. So rave on, Precious!

Miss Common Sense, a.k.a. Earth Mother

Unlike Precious, there was another little girl with uncanny common sense who followed her mother or grandmother around, wanting to do what they did, for they were her role models. This precocious little girl evolved into Earth Mother, the one with an abundance of common sense and logical answers to questions asked. Earth (she becomes Earth Mother later) is gentle and kind and quick to learn. She learned at an early age that vinegar was the best cleaning product because it did not have harmful chemicals, and she knew to sweep before dusting the furniture, otherwise, the broom would stir up more dust. And she knew that you always, always, wrote thank you notes within one week after receiving a gift or act of kindness. She also knew to be polite to adults and say, "Yes, Ma'am" and "Yes, Sir" and "No thank you" if offered a second helping. Earth was and is the epitome of excellent manners.

Of utmost importance to Earth was her ability to do well in school. She was expected to do well, and she did. Her teachers loved her, as did her classmates. Earth always brought home 'A's' on her report card. It's no wonder that she got a scholarship to the school of her choice, which was the Mississippi University for Women, where good Southern girls went to enhance their skills and learn to live and prosper in a crowded world. Indeed, Earth was and is proud to be a "W Girl," even though the venerable school is now co-ed.

Earth Mother as a grown Southern woman is compassionate, dependable, and always the first on the scene in times of need, whether that need is a shoulder to cry on or a wedding to help plan. Count on her to be there with her organizational skills and plain old common sense and good judgment. She is loyal, protective of her friends, and a true gem. Earth is the girl you'd want your only brother to marry, for she does indeed possess the wisdom of the ages and would be a terrific addition to any family. Earth is a great favorite Southern woman very much in demand as a volunteer, community activist, and all-round best friend.

Miss Tom-boy/Mrs. Good Wife

Those adventurous girls who were the most athletic and daring were known as tom-boys. Tommie was a cute, outdoorsy girl who could fish, hunt, and shoot with the best of them – the best of the boys, that is. She was also competitive, and was better at most sports than many of her male counterparts. Once when the boys wouldn't let her play football because she was a girl, Tommie sat her stubborn little self in the middle of the football field and would not budge. The boys were afraid to play over her because she might get hurt and would later seek revenge. Woe unto them should that occur, so the game abruptly ended and the boys went home.

As an adult, this tom-boy turned gorgeous Southern woman instinctively knows how to cook the quail, venison, and wild turkey so that it's the tastiest ever. In addition to these innate skills, Tommy can birth the babies and entertain her husband's hunt club cronies, and accomplish both with style and finesse. Rumor has it that tom-boys make the best wives, and they are not high-maintenance as Daddy's darlins' are wont to be. Tommie likes nice things, but she doesn't pout if they aren't readily accessible.

Tom-boys are perennially cute and tailored, and whether she works outside the home, or in, or both, Tommie is a woman of substance. She carpools, does exemplary Junior League work, volunteers with the Humane Society, and attends church regularly. Her husband is the lucky one, because she can do most anything and does so without complaint. We hope he appreciates her many fine qualities.

If Tommie remains single, count on her to have a fabulous career, because she will give it all she's got and she won't back down from any challenge. This fearless leader sets the standard for others to follow.

Miss Wild Child/Ms. Wild Woman

Trust me when I tell you that wild women were once wild little girls. Wild Child would do anything on a dare, things that would make others dizzy with fright. She was smoking behind the garden shed at the early age of 12, and raiding her parent's liquor cabinet a few years later. Wild Child didn't particularly like to drink, she just liked the idea of doing what was forbidden.

Here's a saying that's come into vogue again recently: "Wild women don't get the blues." Probably because they're far too busy having a good time. Much too soon, our Wild Child becomes a Wild Woman and she continues along her path of wreaking havoc on the nerves of those near and dear to her. She quit college to pursue a career in the theatre, and guess what, she made it. To date, she's been in a couple of Broadway plays and is on her way to Hollywood, we hear.

Luckily for Wild Woman, her wildness meant letting her hair down and having a good time. She never lost control of her faculties and remains one of the most disciplined people we know, once she commits her energies to the project at hand. That trait just may make her a household name. We hope so, for it's the wild women of the South who contribute to the *lagniappe* (a little something extra) we so much enjoy.

The South is a haven for wild women, and sometimes the wildness gets better with age. As Southern women begin to lose the dew of youth, they usually incorporate the next best thing: the confidence to be a bit on the wild side in speaking their minds.

And remember, there's a distinct difference in "wild" and "wicked." Wild is fun and frivolous…wicked is mischievous, and should be watched more carefully.

Miss Wayward/Ms. Wicked

This one can be a bad girl. She was the little girl who found bizarre ways to get even with anyone who had the audacity to go against her wishes. She was not totally bad, for Miss Wayward was very loyal to the people she loved, though they were few in number. She was selective to a fault, and often chose only those friends she could dominate.

Wayward/Wicked grew from girlhood to womanhood, and her reputation followed her growth cycle. She would take it upon herself to right a perceived wrong. Once, Wicked was told of an unflattering remark made by one of her few chosen friends, and to get even, she released two pounds of catalpa worms in the friend's car. Another slight was settled with an ice pick, which she used to puncture all four tires on the slightee's car. But she would engage in the same mischief for her friend who had been slighted, because she was, after all, loyal to those she loved.

As an adult, Wicked was the ring leader in seeking revenge on a woman who had seduced the husbands of two of her friends. They decided that the low-rent, homely, woman must be a pepper hot sex addict, so they planned a way to get even. What they did —and this is supposed to be a true story— was pretend to befriend her by asking her to go shopping with them. Once they got her in the car, Wicked and the women headed to a vacant house in the country, spread-eagled the vixen, and proceeded to generously saturate her private parts with a box of cayenne pepper. They left her there to get home the best way she could. Vixen and her cuckolded husband soon moved from that small Southern town to parts unknown.

Wicked has calmed down considerably, but she's still treated somewhat skeptically by other than her few loyal friends. Those who knew her "back when" aren't sure when her wicked ways will reappear. The general consensus is don't get on her bad side and you won't find out.

Miss Flirt/Ms. Vamp

We've all known them…pretty and prissy little girls who instinctively knew how to flirt. They first honed their skills on the physician who delivered them, if the attending was a male, and they perfected those skills playing doctor with the boy next door. Even from toddler days, when a man entered, our girl Flirt went into action. Her luminous eyes commenced to sparkle, her little chin slightly dropped so that she could gaze up into his eyes through her long lashes, and the mysterious smile appeared. That smile! She smiled as though she was the keeper of all the scintillating secrets. In no time, the resident male was smitten, and Flirt was in her element.

In school, the other girls avoided her, because they'd as soon keep her away from their boyfriends. The Precious at her school was particularly mean to her, so Flirt became a loner with no close girlfriends, except for one or two Plain Janes who had no boyfriends for Flirt to steal. Actually, the Janes loved being in her presence because that's the only time boys came around. Indeed, Flirt was a honeycomb to the bees, and she reveled in the attention.

As a full grown Southern woman now known as Vamp (Flirt 'developed' at the age of 13 and went into full-fledged vamp-dom at that time), she can be seen all over the South, from Dallas to New Orleans to Atlanta and most points in between, always in the center of a group of men. Vamp is a traveler, actually her career is in the travel industry because that's where she meets the men she likes. Doctors, lawyers, and executives travel, and that's what Vamp wants: a handsome, well-educated, successful man who can keep her in penthouses and Porsches. She thought about vamping Donald Trump when he split with his Georgia Peach, but his hairstyle just would not do.

Yes, Vamp is out there, strutting her stuff and making men drool. It is all by design, for she knows the impact she has on men, and she uses it to full advantage. As an adult Southern woman, Vamp is not as pretty as some, but what she has is plain, old-fashioned sex appeal with a magnolia-dripping Southern accent. She especially turns it on with Ivy Leaguers who are saps for softness and femininity. Her voice is so well modulated it has a sexy, whispery quality, and men love that, too. She'll find her man and marry well. She's counting on it.

Vamp will come back home to her 20th high school reunion and be the envy of everyone there, with her diamonds and designer clothes and the best address in the biggest town. Precious will be nicer to her now that she's rich, and Vamp will act as though she doesn't remember who Precious is. Indeed, pay back is hell. Vamp, however, maintains a certain generosity to people she considers kind, but Precious does not fit that category.

If the reunion has one evening that's relatively dressy, watch out. Vamp, Precious and Wild Woman will by vying for attention. They've known each other a long time, and deep down, they really do admire each other, but don't let one look better than or younger than the other! Yes, girlfriends, these are the women that keep us on our toes and keep attention riveted on Southern women!

"I love my past. I love my present. I'm not ashamed of what I've had, and I'm not sad because I no longer have it."

— Colette

Checking out the competition.

10

TIPS
How to be the Most Fabulous Southern Woman!

1. Speak proudly about where you're from because anyone worth knowing knows that the South is truly special.

2. Brag about your alma mater, if it's a good Southern school. Otherwise, listen, ask questions.

3. Have a dinner party and use old sterling and fine china (even if you purchased it at an antique shop), and have food served by a server dressed in a starched black and white uniform, if possible. Wear a strand of pearls.

4. Be well-informed on current affairs. The impression that Southern girls lack intelligence has to go! Be prepared with a few zingers…about the arts, politics, history and such. Leave no doubt that you're well read. Be sure to be familiar with and talk about Southern women writers, many of whom are represented in this book.

5. Bring up the subject of travel. Tell a funny anecdote about something that happened to you in Europe, if it did. If it didn't, be careful. So many people now travel, you may get caught in an inaccurate description of something, and that's not good.

6. Above all, be gracious and hospitable, for that's the Southern way. Remember that if all else fails, a Southern woman still has her manners and her poise, and many have an inbred sense of style and grace. Use those attributes wisely and well.

WELL-BRED SOUTHERN GIRLS...

- ...Would not be caught dead in white shoes after Labor Day.
- ... Do not smoke in public.
- ...Show respect for their elders, especially grandmothers who may someday bequeath them the family heirlooms.
- ...Always call their fathers' "Daddy."
- ...Have mothers and grandmothers who ask all their boyfriends, "Who are your people? Where are they from?"
- ...Accept genteel poverty as though it's an honor, but don't feel much compassion for people they consider "low rent."
- ...Are highly suspicious of men with tattoos, but women with tattoos, well, that's just too much to fathom.
- ...Have an appreciation for the arts. They love the theater and any play that has Tennessee Williams' name on it.
- ...Pretend to be sweet little things to make their Mama's proud, but let them loose in New Orleans, and watch out! These Southern sweeties know a thing or two about letting the good times roll! And roll, and roll, and roll.
- ...Never stray too far off course. They usually do what's expected, for that's the Southern way. For the most part, that is.

CHAPTER 2

A Good Man is Hard to Find

Flannery O'Connor

Flannery O'Connor was a Southern writer whose work won critical acclaim before and after her death. Born in Savannah, Georgia, in 1925, this devout Catholic girl kept journals, wrote poems and short stories in her childhood. She was a naturally gifted writer who graduated from Georgia State University, attended the Writer's Workshop at the University of Iowa where she earned her MFA, then lived in New York City and Connecticut for a time. During those brief years, her work was published in *Accent, Mademoiselle, Sewanee Review,* and *Partisan Review.*

In 1950, at the age of 25, O'Connor had her first attack of lupus, the disease that claimed her father's life when she was 15. From that time on, she lived with her mother on a farm near Milledgeville, Georgia, and she continued to write. Her first novel, *Wise Blood,* earned impressive reviews but its theme left reviewers somewhat puzzled. One critic compared her to Kafka.

Miss O'Connor continued to publish short stories and another novel, *The Violent Bear It Away*, which was filled with religious symbolism. She loved to write short stories and loyal readers loved to read them. Among her most acclaimed were *A Good Man is Hard to Find (1955)* and *Everything That Rises Must Converge (1965),* the latter of which was published after her death in 1964.

Finding That Good Man

Southern women know that a truly good man is indeed hard to find, but finding one is not impossible. Once he's found, keep him close, because with the ratio now three women to every man, there's someone waiting in the wings. Remember Ms. Vamp? She's the leader of the pack, so now that you're more aware of the competition, you know what to expect.

A good man will not be found if the woman sits at home, unless he's a repairman who comes to her house, and those guys are usually married with a passel of kids. So it's up to the woman to find out where the men are, and go there. But be selective. Look at the places where responsible men go. If his place of choice is a racetrack or casino, more than likely he's a gambler and not a good risk. If he's met through the personal ads or online, ask this question: if he's as terrific as he says, why is he trolling for women this way? If a man is met at a bar, can the woman be certain he's not a married man in town on business? Not every man has stellar character, so women must be aware that flaws exist and try to avoid men who have obvious ones.

We hear that some men, surely the worst of the lot, are married and will not admit it. One lovely and exciting Southern woman we know —who was no novice in the ways of men— met, dated, and became engaged to a supposedly wonderful man. Her only concern was that he never took her to meet his parents, who lived in the same Florida city, and never invited her to his home. She was perplexed and when she asked about it, he always had an excuse: his parents were on a cruise, Mom was not feeling well, his apartment was being redecorated, blah, blah, blah. Later, while speaking with him on the phone, she heard a child say something and then the word "Daddy." She asked him about that and who the child was. He came up with a lame excuse. She knew he was lying and the truth finally came out. He was married! His wife worked nights as a hotel manager, he got sitters, and hit the trail looking for pretty women. He never saw that pretty woman again, nor the 'engagement' ring he'd given her. At least she salvaged something from the embarrassing situation and learned a lesson: If something seems awry, it usually is.

Of course, many factors determine the approach one takes in finding a good man. If the man is known through work, she'll know more about him and know whether or not he's sincere. If he's a complete stranger and what he says just doesn't ring true, she may want to do a little detective work. One resourceful Southern woman tells us that she uses her acting skills to check him out at his workplace. She calls and asks for someone in personnel to verify information about an employee. She pretends to be a loan officer at a bank and she needs to verify information for a car loan applicant. She asks his correct name, his title, salary range, years employed, address, and number of dependents. If he has dependents, he's either married or divorced. If the personnel person won't verify, our friend acts very indignant, says she'll reject the application, and hangs up. She says that her detective work is not lying, exactly, it's merely using unorthodox methods to protect herself and prevent future pain and anguish. This is a wise woman, and perhaps a little bit wayward, too.

Widows are in a special category. Recent widows need time to mourn, and for some, that time may be lengthy. Not every widow wants another man. Some think they've had the best and aren't interested in the rest. But others can't stand the loneliness and want to find another mate as soon as possible, after an appropriate mourning time, of course. What does widow do when the time is right? She becomes observant and watches for men without a partner. To get his attention, she asks directions to some obscure place, perhaps an art gallery or theater in the adjoining town. If there's any interest on his part, the question should open a bit of dialogue, if he's smart. If he's not smart, she's probably not interested, anyway. Ms. Wayward says, "Run..."

The woman who's looking to meet a good man has many options: she goes to church and joins a singles Sunday school class; she joins a Y or gym, or a singles club that takes trips. Unless she's on a strict budget, she takes a cruise or two to foreign ports. If money is tight, she becomes involved in local charities as a volunteer; she takes continuing education classes; she joins a book club; she goes to the library to read *The Wall*

Street Journal; she attends her class reunions. And she tells her friends she's interested in meeting single men. Qualify that with GOOD single men. Precious usually knows good men, through her husband.

So she's met him, he's legitimate, and they're on the first date. Most women love attention, but on the first few dates, he must be the focus. She listens; asks questions; lets him know she's interested in him – and all the while she's interested in learning if they may be compatible. Our Southern wise women *confidants* say that if they are not compatible, do not pursue this relationship because it can only lead to frustration. Sounds like good advice, perhaps it's from the ever-sensible Earth Mother.

Our wise women also say, "Don't rush into anything." Whether the woman is divorced or widowed or single by choice, she can have a full and active life without the constant companionship of a man. One suggestion is to find a group of girlfriends to go places with, and plan a road-trip or two. Even if it's dinner out one night a week, it can be fun. "And if a woman's libido is upwardly mobile and decent single men are scarce, be creative," according to Ms. Wayward, who was a big fan of the HBO show "Sex in the City."

It seems that certain women never tire of looking for a mate, for they do not feel complete without a man. Some of the senior ladies read the obituaries in the local newspaper to see what woman died and left a widower. They look up the address, and two weeks or so after the funeral, the lady appears at the grieving widower's door with a tasty casserole and cake, or perhaps a full-fledged meal. She says, "I told your sweet wife I'd look out for you, and here's some food. Shall I come in and serve it for you?" *Viola!* The romance is about to begin. He's so lonely and so glad to get good food, he forgets to ask how she knew his late mate. I personally know of at least three cases of the "casserole and cake lady" who married the widowed husband. Some of their recipes are in the last chapter of this book.

Not every woman is a candidate for marriage. Some prefer to remain single for life, and what's wrong with that? The idea of having male "friends and lovers" has merit and advantages, if both partners feel comfortable with that situation and if they are self-sufficient. If any woman does not possess a modicum of self-sufficiency, she'd best make acquiring some a top priority at this time in her life.

Southern women have not survived this long without being strong and able to handle whatever comes their way…from the Civil War to the Great Depression to the inherent changes in society…some of which the Southern sisterhood wish could be un-changed. Among the things that warrant change: a lapse in manners and dress. Who wants to see the buttocks of boys whose jeans are too low? And who cares to glimpse the privates of girls who wear fabric that was once denim and is now full of holes? Sophisticated Southern women wager that some video queen started the holiest of holes trend. They think it's tacky, which is their opinion and may not be yours. They are merely exercising the option to speak their minds, which is one of the positive things about being a Southern woman, especially one of a certain age. And don't we all get older every day?

Yes, we do have the right to say what we think now that "political correctness" has finally run its course, thank God. And surely, the shabbily-dressed and unkempt people have the right to dress that way, but in some cases, it is offensive and down-right nasty, as when something that looks suspiciously like toilet tissue attaches itself to the top of those low-riding jeans. This would not be the intended spouse you'd want your child to bring home to Mama. Now be truthful. Would it?

Flannery O'Connor had the right idea that a good man is hard to find, but the way Southern women see it, nothing is impossible. They say, however, not to appear too anxious, for Southern women learned at an early age that men are hunters by nature. Let them think they've done the hunting and bagged the top prize: YOU. And that's a comment from our girl Tommie.

TIPS
On Finding a Good Man

1. Join clubs and activities where good men congregate…a health club or spa, an alumni group, a political organization, a country club, a singles club through your church, an investment club, any volunteer organization that has male appeal.
2. Learn and become proficient at sports – at least one. Take golf lessons, tennis lessons, learn to play hand ball, take up fishing, hiking, or biking.
3. Take bridge lessons and learn to play well. Get your master points and go to bridge tournaments. This takes some time, however, so get busy.
4. Tell your friends to introduce you to good, eligible men they know. With about 50 percent of marriages now ending in divorce, perhaps an old fraternity brother or classmate of their husbands is now single. But emphasize *good*. Not just any Tom, Dick or Harry will do.
5. Enroll in interesting adult education classes at the nearest university. Some offer instruction in home repairs, car repair, advanced computer technology, scuba diving, mountain climbing, and the list is endless. Lifetime learning is the best way to meet men of similar interests.
6. Take a trip. Dine at a sidewalk café in Paris or Rome and read *The New York Times* or *The Washington Post*. They're available at good hotels. This will send the message that you're a savvy American, which appeals to both Americans abroad and locals. Interested men will strike up a conversation and our Southern women will welcome the opportunity to engage the man in conversation. He will be charmed before he knows it, and these girls just may bring a European man home to meet Mama.
7. Whatever the situation Southern women find themselves in as they seek ways to meet men, they remain somewhat elusive. They are friendly, always, but they do not appear too anxious to see a relationship develop (key word: "appear"). And that's what makes men want them, according to our wise women.

"Pay attention to character. It cannot be bought, traded, stolen or sold. Remember that character is much easier kept than recovered."
— Tommie

"Men are like fires. They eventually burn out if unattended. Stoke that fire, girlfriend!"
— Vamp

A Southern summer afternoon...the author and her big sister waiting for Brother to finish his flying lesson.

CHAPTER 3
A Member of the Wedding
Carson McCullers

Carson McCullers was born Lula Carson Smith, in Columbus, Georgia, in 1917. The daughter of a jeweler, she began piano lessons at the age of five and later won acceptance at Juilliard, though she never enrolled because she lost her tuition money. She later worked odd jobs in New York City while she studied creative writing at Columbia University and began submitting to magazines in about 1936. In 1937, she married Reeves McCullers, also a writer but not a successful one. They separated in 1940, after both had experimented with homosexual relationships, but they remarried in 1945.

After World War II, Carson lived mostly in Paris. She was depressed and attempted suicide in 1948 and her husband killed himself in a Paris hotel in 1953. During these years, her closest friends were Tennessee Williams and Truman Capote; they all had Southern roots. She and Tennessee were especially close.

As a novelist, she wrote about small-town life in the South. Many of her characters were lonely people disappointed in themselves and the world. In *A Member of the Wedding,* a 12-year old girl feels awkward at her brother's wedding. Adapted to the stage in 1950, the play won the New York Drama Critics Circle Award and became a film in 1952. In addition to *A Member of the Wedding*, her best known works were *The Heart is a Lonely Hunter* and *Reflections in a Golden Eye*. She twice received a Guggenheim Fellowship.

Perhaps McCullers's bouts with depression stemmed from a series of illnesses. She had rheumatic fever as a teenager, which resulted in other health problems, including strokes and confinement. She died in New York City in 1967 after a stroke and brain hemorrhage.

"Woman knows what man has forgotten, that the ultimate economic and spiritual unit of any civilization is still the family."

- Clare Boothe Luce

"Far away there in the sunshine are my highest aspirations. I may not reach them, but I can look up and see their beauty, believe in them, and try to follow where they lead."

- Louisa May Alcott

Men, Marriage, Sex

Some men --not too many, we hope-- are masters of the double standard. They want to "do it" (and you know what "it" is) with every girl they date, yet they want the girl they marry to be virtuous. How can that be? If all the girls have "done it" because of the pressure applied, how can they expect one to be as pure as the driven snow? Not many are these days, unless they're the smart ones who've made a commitment to themselves to wait for marriage to enjoy its sexual largesse. That's a wise decision, girlfriend – then you won't have to deal with or worry about the consequences of indiscriminate sex, not the least of which is pregnancy, STDs, AIDS, and other underlying medical problems that may not occur for years.

This is where the strength of a Southern woman can show its worth. She can just say NO. If she opts for NO and her man of the moment tells his friends she's either frigid or a lesbian because she wouldn't do it with him, her wicked streak takes over. She laughs, and tells them that she's never been a fan of peanuts. Let them form their own conclusions. She's saved face, he looks like the jerk he is, and she can make up her mind to reserve the right to be selective, or wait for marriage. It is HER choice.

So regardless of whether or not she waits to engage in "it," our girl has chosen the right man and the wedding bells are about to ring. Weddings are big business down South, and the irony is that about half of the weddings now end in divorce. The parents spare no expense in getting their girl wed, for it's an important occasion, no matter the ultimate outcome. Huge weddings are traditional, and old Southern families are death on tradition. Precious, Earth, and Tommie are especially well-versed in tradition, and they all had major weddings.

Woe be unto the bride who wants a small, quiet affair when her mother has been planning that wedding since the day daughter dearest was born. Mama usually wins, and after a series of hissy fits and threats to elope, the wedding plans evolve. If it's to be a big traditional wedding with eight or more bridesmaids, perhaps a consultant should be hired. Otherwise, the mothers of the bridal couple may never speak again after trying to coordinate so many details. Following is a quick list of things to be considered in order of occurrence, but the best suggestion is go to the bookstore and buy any one or two of a plethora of books telling how to create a perfect wedding, or hire a consultant. Precious suggests the latter.

    Now is the time for the engaged couple to meet with both families and decide on a date, place, and a preliminary guest list since the number of guests determine the location and cost for each event. Generally, the bride's family (or the bride if she works and wants to use her own money) pays for the bridal gown and trousseau and most everything pertaining to the wedding, from the flowers to the reception. The groom's family (or the groom himself) picks up the tab for licenses, blood tests, his attire, the rehearsal dinner, the minister's stipend, and the honeymoon. Where will the happy couple live afterward? That's a top priority and a decision that usually hinges upon where the jobs are.

    Along with the items above, myriad ancillary things must be attended to, and the wise woman knows to start with a master list and check-off each item as it is addressed or accomplished. First, select the wedding gown and colors for the bridesmaids, to be enhanced by appropriate flowers. And then the work begins…

1. Reserve the place for the rehearsal dinner and the wedding and reception; confirm the dates with the clergy and the musicians. Book the photographer and videographer.

2. Ask friends to serve as bridesmaids, and let them know if they need to pay for their attire. Tell them where to get the dress, where to have it fitted/altered, and where to get dyed-to-match shoes.

3. Have the invitations printed and addressed in perfect calligraphy.

4. Schedule the transportation from the site to the reception; decide on the menu for the rehearsal dinner and the reception; select caterer; order food and drinks; select and order wedding cakes.

5. Get gifts for the attendants; select and order all flowers and greenery (to decorate site, bride's bouquet, bridesmaids' bouquet, corsages, boutonnieres).

6. Have medical tests, get marriage license.

7. Decide on lodging for the wedding party and out-of-town guests; make reservations for the honeymoon. Need passports?

8. Everything scheduled should be in writing, with copies to all concerned. This can save last minute headaches and guesswork.

The items above are bare-bones things to be addressed if the wedding is to be a big one. The verdict is still out as to whether such a wedding is more important to the bride or her mother. Before the wedding day, expect tears, tantrums, harsh words and hair pullings. Prior to the actual nuptials, most girls will say they wish they'd eloped, but on the day of the big event, as she walks down the aisle on her Daddy's arm, with the handsome husband-to-be waiting for the transition from Daddy to him, she thinks it the most important day ever. And there sits Mother, eyes shining from tears of joy and pride, perhaps thinking to herself, thank God it's over.

It's after the big wedding that the real organizational skills come into play. Plans must be made to return duplicate gifts, exchange according to the bride's preference and needs, and when gifts cannot be exchanged or credited because the place of purchase is unknown, the bride devotes a special closet in her new home for "re-gifting" items. Let's hope another lucky bride doesn't get the same gift she gave! We have it on good authority that one new Mrs. in the Deep South had a large family, plus Daddy's business associates and clients, and she ended the gifting season with huge credits at several bridal registry shops. The girls who choose to elope miss out on the bridal-gift largesse. On a positive note, some run-away brides say that they come out way ahead on sanity – and they don't have a storage problem for surplus gifts, so there are always pros and cons.

Not to worry. Not every Southern family goes to such lengths to get daughters married off. Small, intimate weddings can be the loveliest. Remember how the late John F. Kennedy Jr. and his bride chose a remote island off the coast of Georgia for a quiet and elegant secret affair? Some prefer the trouble-free style and glitz of Las Vegas, where all they have to do is get a license and say, "I do," while others want a completely private affair where a judge or justice of the peace presides. The bridal couple must decide, and the choices are indeed plentiful. It is generally a matter of preference and/or economics.

Small and private weddings are easy, lovely, and the marriage is just as valid without the hassle. If it's at the church or home, just be sure it's elegant and special, Mama. If the reception is in a private home, have beautiful fresh flowers throughout, a violinist or harpist on the premises, great food served on good china with sterling flatware and the appropriate crystal goblets. This sounds like a perfect solution, says Ms. Vamp.

The wedding night has finally arrived, and let's hope it is truly special for the couple. Even if the bride knows the ins and outs of sex because she's been around the block a time or two, a good Southern girl will let the groom lead the way. If he is not too experienced and something is not quite right, she can get a copy of the *Kama Sutra* and discreetly leave it out for him to see, saying she bought it for her own use, inexperienced bride that she is. Ms. Wild Woman says this works every time.

Our wisest Southern women tell us to reiterate that marriage is a commitment that takes a lot of maturity and give and take. They said to remind the new bride that she wanted him, she got him, and now she may have to work to keep him. Remember... Ms. Vamp is watching and waiting!

Wise women also say that it's not all that hard to make a marriage work. Meet him halfway, treat him as you want to be treated, do a few things that are expected and some that aren't, keep looking good, and it's not likely he'll look elsewhere. However, if he turns out to be one of those incorrigible run-around guys or if he's a verbal or physical abuser or even a consistent liar, the advice is to pack his bags and find the meanest divorce lawyer in the state, one who has a proven track record. This is not to advocate divorce because marriages can be wonderful, but women don't have to stay in those that aren't. Some of our senior sisters elaborate more on this topic later in the book.

Perhaps it is not wise to expect perfection right at the start, but give it time. Love grows. Sharing a life with another person is challenging, but what Southern woman doesn't like a challenge now and then? And so do men! They do not like doormats, so don't be one. If they want a Stepford wife, let them buy a robot.

Ms. Wicked's theory is that most men are bored with women who are always drippy sweet and submissive. So speak up! If he's smart, he'll respect you for it, and perhaps come to terms with the fact that you can't be taken for granted. "Show a little spirit on occasion, but don't be a harridan," said Tommie.

Of course, there's a difference in being a Southern woman who's sassy and just a little bit wicked and the wicked witch of the west; the mean kind. If a woman becomes too witchy, remember that Ms. Vamp is waiting in the wings, and she might take advantage of the situation. In deference to Vamp, Wild Woman says that going after married men is not Vamp's style. She'd rather not, but she also believes that if the marriage was what it should be and the man was not a chronic run-around, Mr. Married Man wouldn't be ringing her doorbell.

The elder sisters advise keeping a few simple rules in mind, one of which is never marry a man with the intention of changing him. That seldom works. If a character flaw needs to be changed, perhaps you should have looked harder and found a man who did not need alteration. Look at the valuable lessons taught by nature...does a leopard change his spots?

Before, during and after the wedding and the garden reception.

TIPS
How to Make a Marriage Work

1. Communicate. Tell him how you feel, then listen when he tells you how he feels. Ideally, you'll reach a happy medium.
2. Acknowledge his viewpoint, then express your own without anger.
    Be considerate. Put yourself in his place on occasion, and expect him to put himself in yours. That's the all-important "give and take."
3. Do not use the charge card, debit card, or check book excessively. If he thinks you're a spendthrift, finances can become an issue and romance begins to wan.
4. Show affection. Most men like to be touched or hugged.
5. Pick your battles carefully, say your piece, then get over it.
6. Keep the romance enhanced in whatever way works best for you. Surprise him. Come home early one day and prepare his favorite meal, complete with candlelight and flowers.
7. Find things that you enjoy doing together, and devote time to doing them. Sharing is caring, and mutual interests can cement a marriage.
8. Practice the religion of your choice. People of strong faith seldom stray.

CHAPTER 4
Rocking Chair Blues
Bessie Smith

This Chattanooga-born performer was America's premier blues singer in the 1920s. She first sang on the black vaudeville circuit in 1912 at the age of 18, and her remarkable talent was discovered and lauded. Known as "The Queen of the Blues," Bessie Smith broke attendance records at performances and sold more than 700,000 records of "Down Home Blues," a number that was precedent-setting back then. This phenomenal success made Smith the most famous recording artist for Columbia Phonograph Company.

Bessie Smith's performance base was the "81" in Atlanta. Upon her return from the vaudeville stage, her show at the 81 was broadcast over radio. A performance in Birmingham, Alabama, literally blocked the streets; in Detroit, her opening caused a near riot.

Smith wrote and sang "Rockin' Chair Blues" in 1925 and made jazz history when she and Louis Armstrong performed W.C. Handy's "St. Louis Blues." She also starred in an early talking picture of *St. Louis Blues*, which was her only film. Her most famous song was "Black Water Blues," recorded in 1927.

The outstanding voice of Bessie Smith was heard on 160 records. She was an original and the highest-paid black entertainer of her time. Louis Armstrong said: "She had music in her soul," while Mahalia Jackson later said that Bessie's music was haunting even when she stopped singing. She stopped, abruptly and too soon, when she was killed in an automobile accident in Mississippi in 1937 at the age of 33.

"Nothing plants a woman's feet more solidly on terra firma than having children. Babies make women want to fight for what's right so the off-spring can inherit a better world."
- Tommie

Birthing Babies

Not every new mother suffers the rocking chair blues, but motherhood changes a woman. There was a time when genteel Southern women had their babies, took two or three weeks of bed rest while Mother or Big Mama took care of new baby and new mother. There was another time, however, when babies were delivered at the end of a long cotton row and the mother went back to her picking or hoeing shortly thereafter. Both baby and mother apparently fared well after the ordeal, barring complications, for most mothers went on to have a house full of little ones.

But in recent years, the more pampered new mother was on her own after a week or so, and for the first time in her life, she understood pure, unconditional love. The miracle of this first baby was just too much to comprehend. How was it possible to love a little piece of humanity so much, she wondered. Of course, the colic and nighttime crying required some getting used to. Back in the day, a few drops of paregoric in a bottle of sugar water disguised the colic and relaxed the baby and all was well. More stringent medical monitoring dubbed paregoric a narcotic and it was summarily taken off the market, though it appeared to have appeased generations of fretful babies.

New mothers would do well to listen to the sage advice of older Southern mothers. They're willing to shed light on raising babies, and it's advice to be cherished. My best advice came from a midwife who'd delivered more than 300 babies. Here's the story. She and I were waiting to have our eyes examined in an optometrist's office in south Mississippi. My husband was in the Navy at the time and I went home to be with my parents in the Jones County countryside. During pregnancy, I read constantly, about three books a week. My parents and grandmother told me not to read so much because I was in a weakened condition and my eyesight would suffer. An old wives tale, I thought. But they were right. Suddenly, after the baby came, words were blurred and I needed reading glasses, which is why sweet, sleeping baby and I were in the waiting room.

The waiting room woman commented on how soundly my pretty baby was sleeping. I told here that was the pattern: she slept all day and stayed awake most of the night. She asked me when I bathed her and I said in the morning, when I dress her for the day. The wise woman said, "Honey, you bathe that baby at night, and she'll be relaxed and ready to sleep for hours."

We continued to talk and I introduced myself, as did she, and she told me she had two children who lived away: a daughter in New York City and a son in the military. Her name was Mrs. Katie Price; her daughter was the Metropolitan Opera diva Leontyne Price. I commented that she must be so proud of her daughter, whose remarkable talent had earned her acceptance at Juilliard and a top position at the Met. Mrs. Price said that yes, she was proud of her daughter, and equally as proud of her son who was an officer in the military, serving his country.

She was a delightful lady, and her advice worked. My little baby girl slept all night from then on. Unfortunately, young mothers today don't have access to such tried and true suggestions, and babies cry. Here's a time-tested tip: babies love tub baths, but only baby-size ones. They feel lost and abandoned in a big tub, so use a small tub or even the kitchen sink, but line whatever you use with a towel or two. Have the comfortably warm water no more than two inches deep, then lower the baby, talking gently for reassurance. Support the baby's head with your wrist, while the hand supports the little shoulder. Continue to talk quietly, and let the baby feel the calming effect of the warm water. After rinsing, wrap baby in a soft towel and gently pat to dry.

One wise and worldly 94-year-old mountain woman in western North Carolina known for her good health and use of herbs and old remedies says this about crying babies: "Keep their feet warm." Aren't we all uncomfortable when our feet are cold? Babies can't tell us, so they fret and cry.

Other suggestions come from a current pediatrician who guarantees success at stopping crying. He says to wrap babies securely in a cotton blanket. First, wrap their mid-section, then position their arms at their side, and tuck the blanket ends beneath the little bodies. This makes them feel enveloped, as in the womb. He also suggests turning the baby on its side or its stomach. If nothing else works, hum in the baby's ear. They are accustomed to noises in the womb, and the humming in the ear will lull them to sleep.

Far too soon, babies become toddlers, and shortly thereafter comes the hard part. Discipline, and how best to manage it. The old saying, probably not entirely Southern, is "spare the rod and spoil the child." That sounds a bit ominous because my mind sees a child being struck with a steel rod, but certainly that's not the intent. It means, I assume, that children need some form of discipline or chaos ensues. Time-outs, sitting in the corner, or being denied privileges work for some children. Others respond better to psychology, while still others know that if they misbehave, the busy little legs will feel the hedge switch. It's up to the parent to decide which approach works best for their child, but old Southern cracker-barrel philosophy is that few people enjoy being around a brat, so don't let a child get away with bratty behavior. It's going to be a hard cruel world for them if they don't learn to get along with others and realize that the universe is not just for them alone.

Parenting today has a plethora of guidelines. The experts advise… "Present a united front." Meaning, it's no longer appropriate to say, "Go ask your father," or "go ask your mother." That can undermine the authority of the parent saying "go ask…" There's so much information – actually TMI — that good common sense must rule. Some experts say "be flexible." Others say don't be too permissive, and never be disengaged. One stellar bit of advice from Tommie is that the best way to have good children is to have happy children.

In the opinion of our Southern mothers who've grown the best kids, the simple rules are to love them, nurture as needed and discipline when necessary, teach them values, and set a good example. They agree that presenting a unified front is best, and the best way to do that is for the parents themselves to communicate.Talk about the kids over coffee when they're out playing; decide on what works and what doesn't with each individual child, and let them be children for as long as possible. They'll have the responsibilities of adults most of their lives.

Everyone wants smart children, but these days, some kids may be too precocious. This story was told to me by a friend in Louisiana: A precocious nine year old asked her mother where she came from. Mother said, "from God." The little girl asked, "Did you come from God, too?" Mother said that she did. The child asked, "And Grandmother?" "From God also," Mother replied. "And did Great Grand come from God, too?" asked the child. The mother said that yes, they'd all come from God. The bewildered little girl asked: "Does that mean that nobody in this family has had sex in all those years?"

Here's another bit of humor, and since this Southern mother had one son who became president of the United States, she must have instilled a strong sense of purpose in at least one of her children. It was said in jest. "Sometimes when I look at my children I say to myself, 'Lillian, you should have stayed a virgin.'"

- "Miss Lillian" Carter of Plains, Georgia

My mother (center) and friends celebrating her 80th birthday in Laurel, Mississippi. L-R: Mrs. Daisy Grant, Mrs. Floye Robbins and Mrs. May Stennett. "Aunt Daisy" and "Miss May" are sisters.

CHAPTER 5

Making a Mark:
Educator Extraordinaire, Exemplary Leader
Mary McCloud Bethune

No one would have believed that the daughter – the 15th child – of freed slaves would become a leader who crossed cultural and racial lines on her way to becoming a seminary graduate, founder of a college, a college president, president of the National Association for the Advancement of Colored People (NAACP), founder of the National Council of Negro Women, consultant to the United Nations Conference, and advisor to U.S. presidents.

Mary McCloud Bethune was indeed an exceptional woman who made all women proud of her accomplishments. Born in Mayesville, South Carolina, in 1875, her dream was to educate herself, which she did, and then establish a school for black girls. When she learned that one was greatly needed in Daytona, Florida, she moved there…"with $1.50 and faith." Using boxes for desks and chairs, Bethune taught her first class of five girls, and then she went door to door seeking donations for her school. She got her funding from private citizens and local businesses and industry.

Her school, Daytona Literary and Industrial Institute, prospered, and became a positive force in the community, just as Bethune became a positive force in the nation. She also started a hospital for blacks and she founded yet another school: the Bethune-Cookman Collegiate Institute for black males.

As a leader of her race when there were so few black leaders and virtually no black women leaders, she was much in demand in Washington and elsewhere. Her common sense, dedication, and integrity followed her activities as she moved in circles once closed to her race and to women.

Mary McCloud Bethune's indomitable spirit represents the best of America, and reaffirms the strength and commitment of Southern women. Bethune died in 1955, but her courage and charisma continues to inspire.

"Teach your children well. The lessons learned in childhoood become the instincts of adulthood."

Confidence and Charisma, Southern Style

Southern women aren't short on confidence, for most of them have been brought up to think that they're the cutest little things on God's green earth. If not the cutest because of, say, buck teeth or freckles, they're encouraged to be the smartest or the best at something. Anything to make them confident enough to compete in a world where winning is everything, say the parents. So girls of the Southland sign up to take piano lessons, voice lessons, ballet, art, tennis, golf, all in an effort to perfect or enhance their natural talents.

Confidence can often be determined by a woman's outlook on the aging process. Aging is not something we embrace because we'd all like a chance to re-live our younger years, now that we know the ropes. But for the confident woman, aging can be the reward for a job well done. I read that someone commissioned a study of the happiest times in a woman's life, and surprisingly, many in the survey said they were happiest between the ages of 60 and 70. Even more surprising: the happiest women were often those who lived alone. That's reasonable, because they have very little stress. No job to go to, no hungry husband to feed like clockwork, no demands. Stress-free people live longer and healthier lives, as we've seen in our own observations.

Each decade can offer perks to confident women. Rather than dreading the 40s, look at them in a positive light: the Fabulous Forties, the Freedom of the Fifties, the Sensational Sixties and the Getting Senile and Don't Give a Damn Seventies. By the age of 70, a woman has earned the right to be cranky and opinionated if she wishes. If someone doesn't like it, does it really matter in the grand scheme of things? What a joy to think that someday, we can be old women at peace with ourselves and others. And it's high time. We've been out there in the work force with car pool and homemaker responsibilities; we've paid our dues, we've now joined the club of "Choices," and we can revel in the knowledge that we no longer have to please anyone but ourselves, for the most part. If there's a husband in the picture, perhaps he can be convinced that we're reaping the rewards of having been such a good wife and mother all these years. Let him order take-out for dinner.

The Choices Club means that we can choose to sleep late, have a second cup of coffee in bed with a good book, take long, leisurely bubble baths, eat a delicious piece of pecan pie without worrying too much about gaining weight. Of course, for health's sake, we don't want to be porkers, but there's something intrinsically unsettling about older women who look too thin. Equally unsettling are those who've had so much facial surgery their eyes have the perpetual look of fright, or their skin is so tight a piece of plastic fruit comes to mind. A little surgical enhancement to look better and feel better about ourselves is one thing; but let's be honest, girlfriends, when is enough enough? Aging is a perfectly natural process, not to be feared or dreaded by women of confidence. It's a matter of accepting the inevitable with wisdom, grace, and we hope, anticipation, so saith Earth Mother.

Surely, not every person was born confident and acquiring it is easier for some than others, but it's never too late to start. Our wise Southern women who are the most confident say to start with one small success, then confidence will begin to build. The only limitations we have, unless they are physical, are the ones we impose on ourselves. Sometimes the only thing to do is just keep on keeping on, and one day, confidence will be a given.

Charisma is not so easy to come by. That's an intangible quality reserved for a special few. Of the Southern women most of us know or know of, perhaps the most charismatic are Oprah Winfrey and Katie Couric, which is why they're television personalities. People who are charismatic have the power to charm and inspire, and that opens the door for a number of Southern women, though not many of them have achieved the celebrity status of Winfrey and Couric.

They, too, have paid their dues. Though I've not had the pleasure of meeting either one of these Southern women *cum* divas of the airwaves, they were born in the South and their stories are pretty much well known by now. Oprah, a native Mississippian, had her share of hardships on the road to success, but perhaps it is true that from crises come strength. Katie's husband lost a battle with colon cancer at a relatively young age, and that was surely a crisis. But both women made the best of the situations presented them, and see how they're prospering now. Would they have done so well without the gift of charisma? Probably, just not on a national scale. They appear to have the will necessary to succeed.

   Someone once said that the difference between success and failure is that one comes from a strong will and the other from a strong will not. This ties in so nicely with the old saying, "I can, therefore, I will." Shades of our girl Earth Mother, who never backs away from anything, and neither does she question whether or not she can do a certain thing. She knows that she can, absolutely.

"Use the talent you possess, for the woods would be silent if no birds sang except those who sang best."

One of our own...an Atlanta friend known for her work in commercial real estate.

Our own entertainer...a native Mississippi story teller extraordinaire!

CHAPTER 6
One of Ours
Willa Cather

Willa Cather was a Virginia-born writer who moved with her family to Nebraska in 1873 at the age of ten. She apparently found a wealth of goodness and pioneer spirit on the frontier, for that was the basis of many of her novels. She later lamented the loss of the great American frontier with the advent of mechanized farm implements. Factories and machines were the agents of change.

Cather was a woman who knew she wanted to write. After graduating at the University of Nebraska, she began her career as a newspaper reporter and progressed to the editorship of magazines. She first published poems and short stories while working as a reviewer for the Pittsburg *Daily Leader*. She served as editor of *McClure's* Magazine from 1906-12, and then she decided to concentrate exclusively on writing fiction; she was 33.

As a writer of fiction, Willa Cather was known as a superb stylist for her poetic descriptions of land and nature. She preferred to write about the early days rather than the decline she saw in the time in which she lived. Cather is considered the foremost and most authentic writer of frontier life.

Of her many fine novels, the one that was awarded the Pulitzer Prize was *One of Ours,* in 1921. In this case, we're using "one of ours" to depict the many Southern women who have forged careers and names for themselves in a world often dominated by men, as did Willa Cather.

Southern Women Exemplified

What a diverse group! Southern women have been glamorized and romanticized since the women of the planter society began to wilt in the heat of a summer sun. The men folk thought them frail little flowers who needed protecting from the elements and most things in general, so the stage was set for these women to capitalize on being "the weaker sex." How mistaken men were.

When Scarlett O'Hara of Tara fairly floated down the stairway at the Twelve Oaks party on her way to vamp the honorable Ashley Wilkes, did she fool Rhett Butler into thinking she was a delicate flower of womanhood? Hardly. He knew all along that Scarlett was a strong and willful survivor who would do whatever was necessary to get what she wanted. But he loved her anyway, for Rhett was one of the few secure men of the day who liked to be challenged by a woman. So long as the challenge did not involve her affection for the wimpy Mr. Wilkes.

And then there was Melanie, the authentic Southern belle who personified the image of gentility. Melanie was gracious, loyal, forgiving, and she truly loved Scarlett. Just as the two fictional daughters of the Deep South were polar opposites, so are most Southern women, but there are a few threads that weave the belles together: willfulness, charm, and ingenuity.

Not all the willful, charming and smart divas of Dixie were of the manor born. Some were known for their ability to carry on — to make do — to work hard for the survival of themselves and often their families. The Civil War, the World Wars, and the Great Depression were especially hard for some women, and then their husbands died in wars or resulting injuries later and there was little insurance to provide for the family. So even the pampered belle had her troubles, and it seems that those who weren't accustomed to luxuries fared better during those hard times. The women called upon their mettle to make ends meet, and most of them did just that. Hats off to those courageous women! Their willfulness and ingenuity served them better than charm.

No doubt, there are strong and courageous women from Up East, the Midwest, the Southwest and the West Coast, but because of the "wilted flower" image perpetuated in books and movies, it seems that people are surprised when Southern women succeed and show a little backbone.

Perhaps the most memorable wilted Southern woman image is from *A Streetcar Named Desire*, when the emotionally fragile Blanche Dubois was carted off to an asylum. It seems that no one considered the fact that she'd lost her gay husband to suicide, lost her parents, her job, her family home, her dignity, and was raped by her sister's brutish husband when sister Stella was in the hospital having a baby. It is any wonder that Blanche was emotionally fragile?

The question is, however, did Blanche survive? The playwright Tennessee Williams promptly ended the play/film as Blanche left the French Quarter with the kindly psychiatrist and this statement: "Whoever you are, I have always depended on the kindness of strangers."

For all we know, Blanche was treated by the psychiatrist without having had the procedures of the day: shock treatments or lobotomies. Perhaps she regained her faculties as a result of the treatment, resumed her teaching career, and lived happily ever after. That's what this writer would like to envision, anyway, and upon her release from the asylum, I'd like to have seen her seek sweet revenge on the oafish Stanley Kowalski, in a way that only wicked Southern women can devise and execute. We hope that during her treatment, Blanche got her confidence back and took on some of the characteristics of our own Ms. Wicked. Stanley would have learned that pay back is hell when imposed by a wronged woman from deep in Dixie.

In real life, Southern women have used their strengths and myriad talents to show the world that indeed, they can hold our own, thank you very much. Many of them are well known in the entertainment industry, medicine, business, the arts, the law, politics, sports, and most every conceivable profession. Here are a few who come to mind, though this is by no means a complete list:

Kate Chopin, that fabulous Louisiana writer who created a national stir with her novel, *The Awakening*, back in the late 1890s, was way ahead of her time. She told women, in effect, to do their thing. Ellen Glasgow of Virginia was also a writer who told women things they seldom heard. The folk artist from around Natchitoches, Louisiana, Clementine Hunter, was born into slavery and later became a painter. Zelda Fitzgerald, an Alabama belle and wife of F. Scott Fitzgerald, who, according to rumor, was the inspiration or the actual writer of many of his works. Helen Keller, the most amazing woman who made a life for herself even though she was blind, was and continues to be an inspiration to people the world over.

And we can't forget Harper Lee, the novelist from Monroeville, Alabama, who gave us the Southern classic, *To Kill a Mockingbird*. Eugenia Price introduced us to Savannah and the Low Country. Margaret Mitchell, the Atlanta writer, started the "belle syndrome" with Scarlett O'Hara and her only novel, *Gone With The Wind*. Tallulah Bankhead, actress, of Alabama; Ava Gardner, actress, of North Carolina; the Pulitzer Prize-winning Mississippi writer Eudora Welty; the esteemed Flannery O'Conner of Georgia; Carson McCullers of Georgia, blues singer Bessie Smith of Tennessee; New Orleans' own playwright Lillian Hellman; Texas golfer Babe Didrikson Zaharais; activist Sojourner Truth, Mississippi novelist Margaret Walker Alexander; missionary Lottie Moon; North Carolina tennis star Althea Gibson; novelist Katherine Anne Porter; novelist Harriette Arnow of "The Dollmaker" fame; Tennessee's Frances Hodgson Burnett, who wrote "The Secret Garden," and the list could go on for pages more.

Southern women today include Oprah Winfrey, who was born in Mississippi, lived in Tennessee, and is now a woman who enjoys worldwide acclaim; Katie Couric, Elizabeth Dole, Lauren Hutton, Leontyne Price, Cybill Shepherd, Deborah Norville, Sela Ward, Shirley MacLaine, Julia Roberts, Faith Hill, Holly Hunter, Ellen Gilchrist, Dolly Parton, Loretta Lynn, Olive Ann Burns, Ellen Douglas, Beth Henley, Diane Ladd, Fanny Flagg,

Florence King, Ellen Degeneres, Delta Burke, Dixie Carter, BritneySpears, Ann Richards, Barbara Jordan, Cokie Roberts, Kim Basinger, Mary Steenburgen, Anne Rice, Bailey White, Maya Angelou, Kaye Gibbons, Mary Landrieu, Courtney Cox-Arquette, Lee Smith, Lillian Jackson, Kathy Bates, Elizabeth Ashley, Stella Stevens, Anne Rivers Siddons, Rebecca Wells, Jan Karon, Sissie Spacek, Bobbie Ann Mason, Rita Mae Brown, Sharyn McCrumb, Joanne Woodward, Nevada Barr, Rebecca Hill, Ann B. Ross, Ashley Judd, Wynona Judd, Rosalyn Carter, Laura Bush — and if memory serves, the threesome of the 1970s who introduced innovative women to television as *Charlie's Angels,* Farrah Fawcett, Kate Jackson, and Jaclyn Smith — all had ties to the South. Surely there are hundreds more whose names are on rosters in the arts and entertainment, not to mention the business moguls. Kudos to the accomplishments of all the outstanding Southern women.

And to the many non-famous women of the South who go about the business of taking care of their homes and families, working in offices or classrooms every day, and volunteering their time to make their communities the best that they can be, we think you deserve recognition, too. Because of your efforts, the world is a better place. You're the ones who may best remember the following quotes that Southern women have heard all their lives…

- "A son's a son 'til he gets a wife but a daughter's a daughter all her life."
- "Pretty is as pretty does."
- "Marry for love but be sure he has plenty of money."
- "Men who marry a pretty package may be disappointed once they open it up."
- "A friend is one who sees through you but still enjoys the show."
- "Rudeness is a cheap imitation of power."
- "Plan ahead. It wasn't raining when Noah built the ark."

- "Action is the difference between why and why not."
- "If you carry a grudge, it soon becomes a heavy burden."
- "The best way to get rid of an enemy is to turn her into a friend."
- "To have a friend, be a friend."
- "Laughter is natural; hate is learned."
- "Your position doesn't create happiness or unhappiness; your disposition does."
- "Learn the basics in life…honesty, cooking, cleaning, balancing a bank account, shopping wisely, dressing appropriately, one or two skills…and you'll always be prepared for whatever comes your way."
- "Don't wait for opportunities to knock on your door. Knock on theirs."
- "Never leave the house without wearing nice underwear. You never know who may see it if you fall or pass out."
- "Do not wear patent leather shoes in winter and don't wear hose with sandals."
- "Be a good, loyal friend and you'll have good friends for life."
- "Don't gossip about your friend or you'll be the next victim of gossip."
- "Smile often and be sweet. Bees are drawn to honey."
- "To lengthen your life, lessen your meals."
- "Diligence is the mother of good luck."
- "Sleep with the dogs and get their fleas…meaning choose your friends carefully."

- "Virtue is more valuable than gold and diamonds."
- "A house without the warmth of a woman is like a body without a soul."
- "Good wives and good crops are made by good husbands."
- "The doors of wisdom are always open."

Author Rebecca Wells at a book signing for her book, *Little Altars Everywhere*. Wells also wrote *Divine Secrets of the YaYa Sisterhood.*

SMART SOUTHERN WOMEN...

- ...Take care of themselves. They know that life is fragile and they want theirs to be the best that it can be. For themselves, and for their loved ones.

- ...Look out for their health. They eat right, exercise, do not smoke or drink to excess, and get all the recommended medical check-ups.

- ...Always seek a second opinion in matters pertaining to health and well-being. They trust their primary care physician, but know that two minds are better than one.

- ...Work in their communities to make them better. Voluntarism is alive and well down South.

- ...Love the classics, but thoroughly enjoy a sexy novel or mystery from time to time.

- ...Had rather eat out, but know how to please the palate of a visiting gourmand when necessary. And they love to set a pretty table!

- ...Operate under the premise that if you know what's in good taste and lapse occasionally, that's OK. It's the not knowing that's inexcusable.

- ...Know that to be taken seriously, speak in a low voice. People listen to a whisper.

- ...Always have in their closets two or three little black dresses, great shoes, and a strand or two of good pearls.

- ...Dress to the nines for the Kentucky Derby!

CHAPTER 7

The Worn Path

Eudora Welty

"I am a writer who came of a sheltered life. A sheltered life can be a daring life as well. For all serious daring starts from within," said Eudora Welty in her acclaimed book, *One Writer's Beginnings.* She attended a woman's college in her native Mississippi and graduated the University of Wisconsin. After a year of business school at Columbia University in New York, the Great Depression was in full force, so she returned to her parents' home in Jackson and lived there until her death in 2001. After stints as a newspaper columnist and a writer/photographer for the WPA, she began writing full time.

As a child, she honed her writing skills as a listener. She told her parents and their friends to "talk." Apparently they talked, she listened, then found her own voice, which she used so honestly and effectively in her fiction. In *The Worn Path*, Miss Eudora told the story of Phoenix Jackson, a black woman of great courage and determination, who overcame many obstacles in her quest to do something good for her grandson. In telling us about Phoenix Jackson, we very subtly learn lessons about life, and perhaps that's why *The Worn Path* continues to be such a favorite.

The inimitable Miss Eudora Welty was a writer who loved the South. She wrote about it with compassion, dignity and humor, a style that won her a Guggenheim Award in 1942, an O'Henry Award in 1942, '43, and '68, a National Book Award for Fiction in 1971, a Pulitzer Prize for Fiction (*The Optimist's Daughter*) in 1973, and the National Medal of Arts in 1987. Additionally, she was the first living writer ever to be included in the prestigious Library of America series, 1999.

Some who knew her considered her solitary and eccentric, but she was neither. She was a writer who loved to write short stories and novelettes, and she relished her peace and quiet. She never married. Her other best known works are *Robber Bridegroom*, *The Ponder Heart*, and *A Delta Wedding*.

A mother waiting for her daughter, a basketweaver in western North Carolina.

Let Us Now Praise Wise Women Who Came Before Us

- Lest We Forget -

In our own Deep South, we get so caught up in past glories because we have testaments to them-- the grand antebellum mansions, the sterling that was buried to keep "the Yankees" from finding it, the jewels sewn in the hems of the ancestral matriarch's petticoats -- that we sometimes embellish the stories. How often do we remember that most of our revered ancestors were humble, hard-working people who chopped their own small crops of cotton and coaxed a winter garden out of little plots of land? Many of them ate hot buttered grits off tin plates instead of being served lavish meals on fine china by the household staff.

Times were hard for about 80 percent of our people, but Southerners have long known that hardship builds character and strength. They learned to make do with little, and often did without so that their loved ones could have more. How many times have we heard, "God doesn't give us more than we can manage."

Manage they did, and manage well. During the Civil War, our foremothers may not have been able to go to the battlefield as women do today, but they fought their own battles by tending the crops, taking care of the sick and wounded, hearing distant cannons and wondering if one of the cannonballs had hit their husband, son, or father. They persevered, and they did what they had to do. One military officer of the day acknowledged that women indirectly fought in the war, just as the men had done. Some women also served as spies for "the cause." They pretended to befriend Federal soldiers so that they could obtain information for their Confederate men. So contrary to popular belief perpetuated by films and novels, not all Southern women back in the day sat on the veranda sipping mint juleps. Our girl Tommie wants us to remember that fact.

Singer Dolly Parton of Tennessee said in a previous quote, "I was blessed with humble beginnings." Many people do feel blessed that they learned independence and strength of character at an early age.

From hard times come good stories, and Southern women grew up hearing tales and family histories. Consequently, they are natural storytellers, memento keepers, family tree tracers, and talkers! They generally file everything away for future use, and then they bring it out as needed.

Old Southern Remedies That Work Today

We often forget that there was a time when Southern women did not have the benefit of doctors in close proximity and there were few pharmacists back in the day. Resourceful women used herbs, liniments, and old remedies to cure what ailed them and their families, and some of those things worked quite well. Many of the remedies came from such far away places as Ireland, brought here by immigrants. African Americans also brought bits of their cures and culture from their native land and passed them along to future generations. There's still talk of casting "spells," as in voodoo.

Another entire genre of folk remedies came from witchcraft and voodoo queens, among them Marie Laveau. She was born in New Orleans in 1794 as a "free mulatto." Marie married Jacques Paris, a carpenter, in 1819, and they were described as free persons of color. They had a daughter also named Marie, born in 1827; died in 1897. According to reports of the day, Marie Laveau was descended from French nobility, and considering her keen intelligence, this fact was not doubted.

Marie and her entourage could be seen at the annual Quadroon Ball in New Orleans, which was a popular event attended by white gentlemen of means who came to procure a concubine. Though not an authentic historical character mentioned in New Orleans history, the infamous Marie Laveau was nevertheless an important part of the folklore of this most European of all American cities. She was the unquestionable "Voodoo Queen of New Orleans." Her tomb in St. Louis Cemetery No. 1 is still visited today.

Those familiar with South Louisiana and the colorful Cajun culture of the bayous will not be surprised if they've angered or slighted someone and find crossed sticks and a circle of salt on their front porches. These, and other signs of "gris-gris," are recognized as present day voodoo practices, though such practices are rare.

And then there's the mojo, or voodoo charm. It's placed in a small sack containing objects such as a strand of hair or other personal items from the recipient of the hex. One practitioner collected fingernail clippings of the person being hexed; another found his cigarette butts for the mojo.

Not many old remedies were based on witchcraft. Most consisted of the plants and herbs used for natural healing, among them the gel from the Aloe Vera plant for burns and skin irritations. The sassafras root was thought to have medicinal powers and "sassafras tea" was taken for colds and flu. Now, however, the word is that sassafras is a blood purifier that can cause liver damage. As a child, I was sometimes assigned the duty of digging up sassafras roots for my elderly grandmother to clean, boil, and make a tea. She also grated and boiled in a cup of water Octagon soap for me to use as a shampoo to keep my blonde hair healthy and white.

Big Mama also told me of an old black woman, "Aunt Dicey," who helped raise her children, and some of the remedies she used. Aunt Dicey had the babies wear "asphidity bags" on a cord around their necks in the winter. It was a pouch that contained dried herbs and potions she believed would prevent colds and pneumonia, both of which could be serious back then. I have never been able to find any information on "asphidity," and I'm not ever sure of the spelling, but I've heard of it all my life. When a cold did occur, Aunt Dicey placed turpentine (pine tar) on the baby's chest, wrapped the chest and back tightly with a boiled cloth and did not remove it until the cold and cough subsided.

More old remedies follow, some having to do with an age-old staple, white or apple cider vinegar.

- For shiny hair: after shampooing, rinse hair normally. For the final rinse, add one tablespoon of vinegar to a cup of cold water. Pour through hair to get rid of soap build up and add shine.

- Reduce puffy, swollen eyes with a damp tea bag held against the eye area.   A slice of cucumber or Irish potato also works.

- Drink the juice of one lemon in a cup of water first thing in the morning before eating or drinking. Lemon juice is a good healer and blood purifier.

- Vitamin A, taken daily during spring and summer, is said to repel chiggers.

- To decrease a dress size in three months, add two teaspoons of apple cider vinegar to a tall glass of water; drink with meals three times a day.

- To relieve itch from insect bites, soak a cloth in vinegar and place it over the bite, or break and rub aloe vera leaves on it.

- To do away with the odor of onion or fish on hands, wash them in apple cider vinegar.

- A bowl or two of vinegar placed in a freshly painted room will dispel the strong odor of paint.

- For prevention and relief of colds, this old folk remedy promises to help: start with a regular teabag; steep, then add two teaspoons each of honey and apple cider vinegar. Drink as long as symptoms occur. Additional doses of Vitamin C is said to enhance the healing process.

- Gargle with one teaspoon of salt in a glass of the hottest water you can stand. This solution helps sore throat pain and congestion; it also washes away irritation by destroying bacteria.

- Boil a handful of eucalyptus (also called "fever tree") leaves for 20 or so minutes. The steam produced will help clear congestion.

Home-made egg nog for people who were "puny" was a given down South. It contained beaten eggs, heavy cream, vanilla flavoring, and a shot of bourbon. If it did not heal you, it surely made you feel better. Another way that bourbon was used for sore throats: melt one or two peppermint candies in lemon juice and about one-fourth cup of water; add one-half to one teaspoon sugar and a dash of bourbon. That works today for singers and media commentators whose voices have to be mellifluous on demand.

See below several herbs that we believe work well to enhance good health. Before beginning any new regimen of herbs, vitamins, or minerals, consult your physician or pharmacist because some may not be compatible with prescription drugs you may be taking, or with other supplements.

1. Sweet **basil** can be used as a poultice to draw poison, as in a bee sting or pimple, from the skin.

2. The herb **echinacea** is said to help protect healthy cells from bacterial attack by stimulating the process of the immune system.

3. **Milk thistle** is believed to help cleanse and invigorate the liver. It contains silymarin, a potent liver-protecting substance. It is said to benefit those with cirrhosis and chronic hepatitis.

4. **Saw-palmetto** berries are said to benefit women with chronic cystitis and it is believed to help prevent prostate problems in men.

5. Chewable **papaya** tablets contain valuable digestive properties and can aid those who suffer heart burn or indigestion.

6. **Acidophilus** tablets, when taken regularly, can improve the function of the intestines and alleviate some of the harmful side effects of antibiotics.

7. **Ginseng** is a stimulant for mental and physical energy; it is also thought to be a preventive and cure-all for such conditions as anemia, arthritis, insomnia, poor circulation, and more.

8. In capsule form, **garlic** is said to lower blood pressure and cholesterol and cleanse the blood of excessive glucose.

9. The herb **pennyroyal** is used to treat colds (as an inhalant) and for the treatment of menstrual cramps if used as a tea.

10. **Chamomile** is a plant possessing antispasmodic properties that also works to dissipate gastric cramps and anxiety.

There are many herbs that are considered dangerous and should be avoided. Among the most commonly known are arnica, belladonna, hemlock, jimson weed, and mistletoe. Certain Ms. Wickeds have been known to concoct a potion of poisons to serve to a man who mistreated them. The intent was to make him deathly ill, though according to rumor, a few unlucky unfaithfuls did not recuperate from the "devil juice." Back in earlier times in certain circles, the secret potion was said to be a dreaded threat that kept most men in line.

In Eudora Welty's earlier days in the Deep South, herbal remedies – not the poisonous kind — were considered appropriate and necessary to enhance one's health and well being; it did hers for 92 years.

"Most Southern writers were produced by a society in which people talk into the night and tell stories."
-Eudora Welty

Two Southern friends enjoying the best of nature in the "Land of Waterfalls," Transylvania County, North Carolina.

CHAPTER 8

Career-wise and Otherwise

The Grimke Sisters

It was most unusual for girls born into Charleston aristocracy to go against the grain and fight for women's rights and support abolition at a time when both were very unpopular causes. The Grimke sisters, Sarah and Angelina, found slavery repugnant though their family owned slaves.

Sarah, born in 1792, and Angelina, born in 1805, left their native Charleston, South Carolina, around 1830 and moved to Philadelphia to join the Society of Friends. The Friends were known for their charitable work. Angelina, the more cause-committed sister, joined the Philadelphia Female Anti-Slavery Society in the midst of mob violence. After her verbal appeals and published editorials against slavery created animosity in the South, Angelina could never return to Charleston. Sarah followed Angelina as the sisters became the first women to join the American Anti-Slavery Society.

They were equally a committed to women's rights, and they worked tirelessly to achieve the goal of equality. Their stance was that women should have a voice in the laws and regulations by which they were governed. The Grimke sisters faced derision and ridicule for publicly addressing any group that gathered. Women did not do such things, people said. The Grimkes did, and their efforts indirectly lent confidence to generations of women who followed their lead, including Susan B. Anthony and the Suffragists who convened at Seneca Falls, New York, in 1848, to plan ways to give women the right to vote.

Angelina married her mentor and fellow activist, Theodore Weld, after which time the sisters and Theodore continued their work, but on a quieter scale. Sarah died in 1873, Angelina in 1879, in Hyde Park,

Massachusetts. The sisters were never invited to return to Charleston, for they were considered radical and entirely too liberal and strident for genteel Charlestonians.

An after work gathering of "Forum" friends.

Woman's Work is Never Done!

Smart Southern women are here, there, and everywhere, in the work force and in the Mommy Brigade. We only hope that since the majority of women work outside the home, they are paid a salary equal to their male counterparts, but we have reason to believe that they are not. According to census figures, women still earn less than men. The female to male earnings ratio is 0.76. In 2000, median earnings for women 25+ who worked full time, year round, with a bachelor's degree, was $38,200. Men, same situation with a bachelor's degree, earned $53,500. How can that be justified? It's a matter of simple justice: equal pay for equal work.

These are scary discrepancies, ladies, considering the fact that about 25 percent of women who work are heads of households, as in single parents. Are they still being told, "Honey, of course John Doe makes more than you because he has a family to support." Let's hope not! If that is being said, exercise your options and do something about it. John Doe probably has a wife who also works, and I'll bet she is primarily responsible for the kids, the housework, the laundry, the shopping, and the cooking. Old John has it made. He's king of the hill at the office and at home, and he's a dinosaur, according to our Ms. Wicked.

Even though men are now helping more with household chores, the major portion of it still falls on the shoulders of the little woman. If the wife stays at home, that's a different story. Her contribution should be taking care of the home and children. In that case, ideally, she should make the nest and he should do the rest, within reason, that is. Both could combine talents to accomplish certain tasks.

In years past, Southern women as a rule were not as concerned with equality as our Northern sisters because it did not seem to be an important issue, perhaps because not as many Southern women worked outside the home. Back in the day of the feminist movement, I heard one brainless belle say, "I don't like this women's lib business because I want men to open doors for me." Gentlemen still do!

> **TIPS**
> **How to Succeed in a Business Environment**
>
> 1. Don't just work hard, work smart. Be on time for every meeting and never miss an appointment. Take notes, then refer to them often.
>
> 2. When you complete a project that you're proud of, let it be known. Present it at an office or board meeting and get the deserved accolades. You deserve the credit for your good work.
>
> 3. If there's a promotion that you want, go after it. Beef up your resume and apply for the position. Don't wait around for the promotion to come to you, for it may not. If someone with less experience or time in grade gets the promotion instead of you, ask why. You have a right to know.
>
> 4. Be professional in looks and actions, and don't be subservient or a sycophant. Women could well make policy, not coffee, unless making coffee is what she was hired to do. And even if that were the case, she could show a little moxie and move up.
>
> 5. Be pleasant and friendly to co-workers but don't get involved in their personal problems or office gossip sessions. Such things can come back to haunt a woman on the rise.

There was a time when women had to work twice as hard as men to be thought of as half as good. That's no longer true, but still, only 12 percent of top executive positions are held by women. Why is that?

There are not too many gender specific career fields anymore, and that's good for everybody. Some men prefer to be stay-at-home Dads, while Doctor Mom brings home the Dom Perignon. Women now have ample choices, and many are choosing to stay home and be with the children, especially if Dad has a job that requires travel. More is expected of the stay-at-home Mom, because she is involved with kids' sports and other activities, carpooling, school volunteering, keeping the house in tip top shape, and entertaining friends and husband's work associates or clients.

      The Grimke sisters of Charleston would be amazed and supremely pleased at the choices women have today. After all, the sisters devoted much of their lives to seeing that choices could someday be possible. Today's woman may not give much credence to the Grimkes and the later feminist movement, but because of women who came before, women today can now make choices without having to apologize for them. I hope women never feel compelled to say, "I'm just a housewife." They are women who have chosen to be homemakers because they and their husbands put a premium on nurturing children and creating a comfortable home. That's important work, and if stay-at-home Moms got paid by the hour, they may well be earning higher salaries than women with high-powered careers. To work or not to work? We hope the choice is yours.

      Many Southern women love to decorate, garden, and entertain, which perhaps stems from a favorite little girl pastime of playing house. The tomboys, however, have learned to do these things out of necessity, though I'll wager that cooking for a crowd is not on their list of favorite events. The girly-girls of the past are now the real queens of décor and haute cuisine, Southern-style. They read all the latest books on decorating styles, fabric, and colors, and they place *Southern Living, Southern Accents,* and *Veranda* right up there with the Bible.

      Some inventive ladies of the South may subscribe to *Town and Country, Architectural Digest, Travel and Leisure,* and *Gourmet*. Hats off to all of them who read because the more they read the smarter they are, and Southern women do need to let the world know that they are smart. The old "beautiful but dumb" nonsense went out with Jackie Gleason and "The Honeymooners" television series. Thank God. There was a time when women tried to hide their intelligence so that men wouldn't be threatened. We have indeed come a long way, and it's way past time, according to the ever-opinionated Wild Woman.

Not every Southern woman wants to live in a rustic old farmhouse with a hint of history even if it has all the comforts of today's lifestyle. But those who do are usually the ones who enjoy finding perfect *accoutrements* at flea markets or antique malls, and they prefer to do their own decorating. Country chic – sometimes French country or English country —is popular down South, and not only does it have the nostalgic appeal of days gone by, it's also fun to find an old house and use creativity and ingenuity to make it perfect for the family of today.

There must be about 20 magazines devoted exclusively to "country living" and decorating, and they're found in Southern country homes and country home wannabes where they're used as idea sources and how-to information. *Country Home* tells the latest on what the current trends are and where to find them, and their art and articles in the magazine make everything look so perfect and easy. Their advice is to use what you like in decorating, and it may be old wicker picnic baskets (also great for storage), pewter, early hand-made tables and chests, quilts, and other things our mothers gave to charities because their modern daughters did not want "those old things." Precious says to save everything in a special storage place in the attic.

Collecting and decorating provide ways to be imaginative and creative, and there's the added benefit of having fun going on antiquing expeditions in the neighboring town or state. Some of the Southern "old country houses" are indeed showplaces of comfort and style, and a tribute to the woman of the house.

We know many Southern designers who go to Europe a couple of times a year to buy antiques and accessories for their clients. The rumor is that if they go to the right sources, they can get fine European antiques and have them shipped across the Atlantic cheaper than they can buy from some big city antique dealers. Some designers and their clients, however, prefer American antiques if they can be found.

In the South, a New Orleans cabinetmaker, Prudent Mallard, created massive furniture that was popular with the mid-1800's planter society. Either he was the most prolific furniture maker, or many people claim to have Mallard pieces that are actually very good reproductions. Mallard's work is represented in many of the antebellum mansions along the River Road in Louisiana and around Natchez, Mississippi. Ask our girl Miss Precious. She is well-versed in the work of Mallard and other Southern craftsmen.

      Women who love high style and luxury want the finest house with the best furnishings and accessories that money can buy. They find and hire the busiest decorator in town, and then the home becomes a picture-perfect palace. The most expensive decorators have the ASID designation after their names, but some of the best we know are those who have the gift of style, which includes a great eye for design, color, and fabric. You'll find more of the latter in the South, and they're generally those same little girls who built playhouses so many years ago. Indeed, they honed their skills at an early age and you see the results of their talents all over the Southland.

      This story was told as the truth. An interior designer was married to a theater director in a major Southern city. One of her new clients asked what her plans were for the weekend, to which she answered: "I plan to watch my husband's play." The client looked stunned, and asked, "How many husbands do you have, and what do they play?"

      That's the wonderful thing about Southern women. They are funny, versatile, clever, creative, and they do what is necessary to be the best that they can be, whether they're in the home or the international marketplace. For certain, they are serious about the impressions they make.

      Many Southern women are fashion mavens. They like Prada and other designers who are now showing a return to "lady-like" fashions. One Southern fashion leader says that it's time for a return to modesty, because too much skin shown takes away a woman's mystique, and mystique is a powerful aphrodisiac. She says it's a pleasure to see old world elegance on the runways now, and that a return to elegance is on the way.

Shades of Coco Chanel and some of the long-gone designers whose fashions are now in high demand as retro.

The Southern fashionista say to wear appropriate, well-made and preferably somewhat tailored clothing, expensive shoes, and good jewelry, and you're in style anywhere. They add a word of caution: unnaturally colored stiff hair, heavy, excessive make-up, and overpowering perfume is out.

Among the Southern sisters of today, Miss Precious would choose *haute` couture* if she did indeed marry well, while Tommie and Earth both prefer casually elegant styles. Ms. Vamp and Wild Woman would probably select more tailored styles for work and hippie chic after work, while Wicked would wear whatever pleased her at any given moment.

When in doubt, think Ingrid Bergman, Audrey Hepburn, or Grace Kelly and the elegant simplicity they achieved, which is ageless. Easy enough, with a little Southern class and sass!

There's much more to Southern style than clothing. Flowers, too, have reputations to uphold. Red roses are the "I love you" flowers; while ivy, in its various forms, means "friendship, marriage," which may be why ivy is popular as wedding greenery. Some genteel Southern ladies love to grow dahlias, which represent "dignity and grace." Zinnia means "your absence is mourned." If daffodils are sent to Southern women, they take it to mean "unrequited love." Ferns are generally accepted as the plants of "sincerity." And any time for any occasion, a nice bouquet of fresh flowers is much appreciated.

"Flowers are nature's way of saying that the world is good."
- Earth Mother

CHAPTER 9

The World I Live In

Helen Keller

Perhaps the woman who deserves recognition and accolades as having been the most phenomenal Southern woman is Helen Keller. She was an inspiration to a world of women, and her life and accomplishments continue to reaffirm that the human spirit prevails. We should include Annie Sullivan in the accolades surrounding Helen Keller, for this amazing teacher taught a blind girl to live.

In 1880 in Tuscumbia, Alabama, the young Helen Keller was born healthy and sighted, but a mysterious illness that she contracted at the age of 19 months resulted in the loss of her sight. Her family catered to her and she became wild and unreachable, getting her way through tantrums and sheer meanness. Family friend Alexander Graham Bell recommended that the Keller family contact the Perkins Institute in Boston, a school with an excellent reputation for teaching the deaf and blind. Thus they hired a 20-year old Perkins graduate, Miss Annie Sullivan.

From the time she arrived at the Keller home, Ivy Green, Miss Sullivan worked to teach Helen the manual alphabet. She finally succeeded, when, at the water pump, Helen felt water on one hand and spelled the word WATER with the other. They both instinctively knew that Helen was about to enter a new life. Helen and "Teacher" learned everything they could in Alabama then went on for Helen to study at Cambridge School for Young Ladies and graduated from Radcliffe College.

With assistance, Helen wrote her autobiography, *The Story of My Life,* which was widely and critically acclaimed. After college Helen and Teacher settled in Massachusetts, Annie Sullivan married teacher John Macy, who knew that Helen was to be his wife's permanent charge. Annie and John helped Helen with her next book, *The World I Live In,* which was another success. Helen Keller did everything in her power to support the cause of the blind as well as women's suffrage.   She traveled across the country to speak and raise funds for the American Foundation for the Blind.

After Annie Sullivan died in 1936, Helen continued to travel for the cause. She became a world figure and the subject of a play, *The Miracle Worker.* The play and film continue to serve as a testament to the incredible reaches of the human spirit. Helen Keller continued her work for the blind until her death in 1968.

"People are always blaming their circumstances for what they are. I don't believe in circumstances. The people who get on in this world are the people who get up and look for the circumstances they want, and if they can't find them, make them."

- G.B. Shaw

Words of Wisdom

Remember, we do have Precious, Wild Woman, Wicked and Vamp out roaming the streets of the South, sometimes creating mischief and mayhem in their wake, but they are lovable, and they are ours. Their antics help make the South the interesting place it is, and they keep us guessing! They may be wild and wicked, but above all, they are wise. Along with Tommie and Earth, they get wiser with age, and it is the wisdom we'll concentrate on now. Helen Keller set the standard, and she was indeed an inspiration.

You'll have your choice of memorable words and phrases, for some have been around since before our grandmothers were born. You'll find brief synopses of stories, one liners, specific quotes about things of importance, and just plain woman talk. Not that Southern women are selfish and put themselves first, but our advisors say the first and best thing a wise woman can do is…

1. **Be kind to yourself**. And that means eating right and exercising, taking care of your health, and resting when tired if possible. It also means getting rid of harmful habits, such as smoking or drinking excessively. Don't worry about minor disappointments or slights, for worry can cause all sorts of health problems and can make you old before your time. Most of our advisors say, "Get over it and get on with your life," but there are a few of the Wicked Sisters whose advice is to get even. "Getting even," they say, gives one a sense of having control over a situation that has caused grief. That is entirely up to the individual, for many women firmly believe that "killing with kindness" is the preferable M.O., and that treating others as you want to be treated works every time. Perhaps it depends upon the religious depth of the woman in question.

2. **A most important aspect** of being kind to yourself, we hear, is "Don't live your life to please others." Please yourself and people will usually be pleased with you. That brings to mind another old saying: "Other people cannot make you happy because happiness comes from within. A happy person is happy

in most any situation."

3. **The senior Southern sisters admonish**: "Do not be a doormat. Speak your mind, but don't be abrasive." A few well-placed and gently-spoken words can be zingers.

4. **In business, surround yourself with people who are smart and savvy.** Do not depend on them to advance your career, but count on them to help keep you headed in the right direction. Recognize and acknowledge the good deeds of others, for people respond to positive affirmation and they appreciate those who bestow it. Good people will make everyone around them look good, too, and the business is sure to prosper. When a business associate does a good deed, reciprocate. It will come back many times.

5. **Be careful not to step on the fingers** of someone holding on as you progress up the ladder. It will serve you well to help them along if you can. They won't forget it. Friends in business are a treasure to behold.

"Is it possible for a married woman with children to head a major corporation or be a top professional in her field? You bet ... smart Southern women can do anything . And if she hires a nanny, a housekeeper, a cook, and a car pool driver, she can have the same advantages as a man ."

Remembering the Wisdom of Southern Women

My dear grandmother told me that back in her day, women didn't have problems with depression because they didn't have time to think much about such things, for they didn't have modern appliances and push-button conveniences. And they talked more. While the neighborhood women gathered once a week to quilt, they sat around the quilting frame about four hours and exchanged ideas, shared recipes and tips, and talked about their problems. Big Mama said that when a weighty problem is shared, its importance is minimized. She cautioned, however, that it's quite possible to share things without betraying personal confidences. For example, as women today are wont to discuss sex openly, the ladies of yesteryear did not. Their belief was, according to Big Mama, that what happened in the bedroom stayed there. They did discuss having babies and the best approaches to take. Most of their children were home births, for they lived in the country, though their husbands did fetch the town doctor to come out as needed.

We may not have quilting circles today, but we have certain people who are our "grounders," or someone who keeps us focused, picks us up when we're down, shares good news as well as bad, and their mere presence reassures us that life is good. Whether it's a spouse, child, parent, sibling, or friend, cherish that person! 'Grounders' keep us on track and they're worth their weight in gold.

"When the door of happiness closes, another opens; but often we look so long at the closed door that we do not see the one that has been opened for us."
- Helen Keller

In discussing our Southern heritage with some of the wise women in this book, we worried that the South was losing its identity. The consensus was that we like our South the way it is…we don't want the cultural gap to close. Perhaps neither do others, for the decline in regionalism appears to be in reverse. Look at the "GRITS" (Girls Raised in the South) business that's sprung up in Alabama. And even on the Internet, there's a pretty hefty category for "Southern Belles." There are books, items, chat rooms, and yes, a little derision, but perhaps the derision stems from the fact that those deriding are not Southern belles.

We like the things that make us different. Who wants to be just another homogenous blend of Americana? The beauty of this country is its diversity, and much of that stems from regionalism and ethnic or cultural differences. We would miss out on so much if we didn't have the Cajuns and their wonderful customs and music, and that's just one example. Each state has its own special blend of customs and culture and famous old quotes that are sprinkled in many conversations down South. In discussing a failed marriage, one maiden aunt will surely say, "Oil and water do not mix," which is her sweet way of saying the couple had been mismatched from the beginning. Our Wild Woman and Ms. Wicked tried to tell them but they wouldn't listen.

Some of the old Southern sayings help remind us of things the dearly departed tried to impart. One that always intrigued me was, "A rolling stone gathers no moss." I was never sure what that meant, but my mother seemed so certain all the times she said it, I hated to show my ignorance by asking for an explanation.

Wise Women on Divorce and Diet

Divorce is a fact of life, in the South and elsewhere, and it's a topic that our wise women thought we should address. We like to believe that all marriages are made in heaven and husbands are gods who grant us the privilege of sharing their illustrious lives. Could that be the result of our childhood story books, among them "Sleeping Beauty" and "Cinderella"? But we quickly learn what's fact and what's fiction. With about 50 percent of marriages now ending in divorce, many of us could use a few survival tips for divorced women.

Becoming a "Ms." after Mrs. will be what you make it. It can be challenging or it can be dreadful, the latter the case if the new Ms. sits around waiting for the phone to ring, expecting Prince Charming to call. The wait may be interminably long if the woman is over 40, for most available, straight, men between the ages of 40 to 60 want a woman in her 30s. And they want her to be sexy, smart, self-sufficient, and they fully expect to be the only man in her life. These newly divorced men, too, may have a long wait, for such women are usually taken or don't want to be.   Smart men look for women of quality, no matter her age, and all he needs to do is look around for they are in abundance. Men have it made, with the statistics now about three women to every man.

Harriet Beecher Stowe was so right when she said, "So much has been said of beautiful young girls, why won't somebody wake up to the beauty of older women?" Tell it like it is, Miss Stowe. IF divorced women want to turn the tables on men who seek youth and find younger and more attractive men for themselves, they would do well to read the French writer, Colette. The story, from the late 1800s, is that she was a former courtesan with a reputation for elegance who, after her working years, taught young men the finer art of love making. The thing was, they all fell in love with her. They loved her honesty, her beauty, her wisdom, her flair, and the fact that she made them feel special.

Colette's short stories, *Cherie* and *The Last of Cherie*, tell about a young man who was so desperately in love with the older woman, he was ruined for anyone else. Even when she was an older woman (late 60s) and he was still relatively young, he loved her to distraction but she sent him away. So, dear friends, it is possible to find young love, and it's even easier now because age doesn't seem to be much of a factor these days.

The first thing after divorce, say the wise women, is to give yourself time to re-group and regain your confidence and self-esteem. If it takes years, that's OK, because during all this time, you'll be getting back in touch with YOURSELF. Learn to like who you are and what you have, not the least of which is the freedom to please yourself. Eat when you're hungry, rest when you're tired, have girlfriends in for cocktails or coffee, and that should help lessen the trauma of divorce.

The writer Toni Morrison said, "The loneliest woman in the world is a woman without a close woman friend." Even if you didn't keep up with your women friends when you were married, it's not too late. Many women would love to get together and go out to dinner or a play or more. Call them! See how much fun you can have with women in similar circumstances. If one wants to sit around and wallow in self-pity, don't call her again. Seek people who make you feel good, because feeling good is contagious.

Once you begin to be pleased with your new life, your attitude will change and others will notice --and proably appreciate-- the new you! This might be the time to get a new hair style, new cosmetics, and maybe lose a few pounds.

Before you begin a diet, speak with your health care professional, though some of the wise women have lost a few pounds by limiting calories. We know that the carb craze is the thing right now, but for most women, counting calories always works, especially in conjunction with about 30 minutes of exercise several times a week and six to eight glasses of water each day.

One thing that worked for most of the wise women who wanted a new look was to consume no more than 1500 calories a day for two or three weeks. The 1500 calorie plan is based on a woman weighing 140 pounds and consuming 2100 calories per day. To lose one pound each week, which is considered safe, deduct 600 calories per day from your intake.

Here's a list of foods and quantities that have 100 calories or less each:

1/2 cup applesauce	30 spears of asparagus	1 medium banana
3 stalks broccoli	2 cups cooked carrots	3 cups raw cauliflower
1 boiled egg	2 peaches	1 orange
1 pear	15 med. boiled shrimp	2 cups turnip greens
1 cup cereal	1/2 sweet potato	2 cups lettuce
2-1/2 cups cabbage	3 Graham crackers	1 cup skim milk
2 slices bacon	1/2 cup canned salmon	1/2 grapefruit
1 c. vegetable soup	1-1/2 slices bread	1/2 cup tuna fish

This appears to be a healthy assortment of food for a limited time diet, and it is an incomplete list. Among the things to avoid if you wish to lose weight is mayonnaise (1 tablespoon, 110 calories, 12 grams fat); peanut butter (1 tablespoon, 86 calories, 7 grams fat); Brazil nuts (4 nuts, 105 calories, 10 grams fat); margarine (1 tablespoon, 100 calories, 11.3 grams fat). One wise woman says that when she wants to shed a few pounds, she avoids anything white…flour, sugar, pasta, rice, white bread. Like most things in life, dieting is a matter of common sense.

If we're lucky, we all have memories of things our mothers told us.
These "Mama Saids" seem most appropriate in this book.

Mama Said…

- …Flowing water never grows stagnant.
- …If we do the best we can, we never know what miracles may occur.
- …People who are honest don't ever have to worry about being caught in a lie.
- …Water seeks it own level.
- …Nothing can bring peace like knowing you've done the right thing.
- …Adversity is an experience that makes us wise.
- …Read voraciously, for books are the true university.
- …To know how to grow old gracefully is the PhD in wisdom.
- …Always remember your manners, for manners are the first inkling that you're a person of quality.
- …Celebrities are people who do everything to get noticed and then wear big hats and dark glasses so they won't be recognized.
- …You can't get a rich husband without the proper setting. Exhibit elegant furnishings, good paintings, and decorative arts. These are the accoutrements that men of means recognize and appreciate.
- …Work on your charm. If you have an abundance of charm and personality, you can get by with little else.
- …Don't EVER be caught without makeup, neat hair, and nice clothes! One never knows who may knock on the front door.

Hospitality, Common Sense and Humor

Southern women are known for their hospitality, and hospitality begins with one simple thing: a smile. Some of the women from across the South have told us a few tidbits of information that we think is right on target, yesterday, today or tomorrow. Here's what a Texas mother told us:

"If you want people to like you, give them a reason. Smile a genuine smile, and be kind. A smile is universal and there are no language barriers. Make it a habit. Smile frequently – it's contagious and will come back to you many times over. Your mood will be elevated and you'll feel a sense of well-being."

Our Dixie divas of a certain age agree that divorce is surely warranted in cases of physical abuse, alcohol or drug addiction, emotional cruelty or abandonment, but wise women who've seen both sides of the issue say that couples might fare better if they viewed marriage as a lifelong commitment. They say there's profound meaning in the words, "For better or worse," and with perseverance, the worst can become the best. Apparently, there's great comfort in growing old with someone you know so well. Unless, they say, the circumstances are indeed extenuating. If so, call a lawyer. Pronto! Preferably a female attorney who has a reputation for winning cases for other women. Even in the law, unfortunately, the old boy network sometimes comes into play and "the little woman" is not taken seriously and therefore not always the recipient of good news in a divorce settlement, warns Precious.

Here's a story that Precious will love. Bayou State friends tell us that Louisiana native Henri Bendel, who earned fame and fortune as the proprietor of Bendel's in New York City, once had a female president who explained the difference in fashion and style. "Fashion says, 'Me too,' and style says, 'Only me.'" Just as Precious loves anything pertaining to fashion, Earth and Tommie are more logical in other aspects of life in the sunny South. Tommie believes that women who can manage pregnancy, childbirth, menopause, and aging while still looking good and being civil can do anything! Tommie and Earth are also the ones who first said "hats off" to the women of vision who had dreams and made them into realities. Earth said they were surely the same women who had great faith and believed that all things happen for a reason and that some good comes from everything.

Humor is important to Southern women. They revel in telling funny stories. This one was told to us by a woman from Florida. "A concerned female lawyer counseling a woman who was filing for divorce said, 'You're 91 – you've been married for 71 years. Why get a divorce now? The woman answered: 'Our marriage has been on the rocks for 65 of those 71 years, but we wanted to wait until the children were independent.'"

As a public service project, a sorority at a major Southern university sponsored a golf tournament to benefit a local child abuse prevention organization. Thousands of flyers were printed that read: "Help Stop Child Abuse by Shooting a Hole in One." This story has made the rounds for years, but it's place of origin has not claimed it.

The following story shows how wise women endear themselves to us. It was told by a woman in Georgia, a friend of the mother. "When my son told me was gay, he waited for signs of my disapproval. I would never disapprove, because a person's sexuality is a small part of who they are – a part that I believe to be a private matter. The hesitation that he mistook for disapproval was concern for his health and well-being. Homosexuality is still not widely accepted, and I was concerned that he may suffer ridicule – or worse — from others. My love for him has never, will never, change because he chose an alternate lifestyle. I love him more than life."

This great idea was told to us by a friend in Mississippi. We'll call it *Girlfriends Unite*. "We planned this unity weekend for months in advance. It was to be at a friend's camphouse on a lake in Alabama. Four friends were each to invite three other friends not known by others. Our aim was to have a modern day 'consciousness-raising' to exchange ideas, visit, and just kick back and have fun for a weekend. There would be 12 of us, the number the camphouse could comfortably accommodate, and that included the use of fold-up beds on the wrap-around screen porch.

"We came from diverse backgrounds across the South; some married, some divorced, two single by choice. Nothing was planned – it was to be a laid-back weekend. Someone brought a big pot of vegetable soup; two others brought salads, others brought fruit, snacks, wine, soft drinks and such. Everyone ate when they were hungry – no formal sit-downs. Sometimes we talked as a group, other times two or three of us went for a walk in the woods or sat by the lake, each group lost in sharing memories and mishaps, and learning from the experiences of others.

"By the time we left on Sunday afternoon, we'd discussed single life in big cities, the quiet life of a small town, careers, the best and worst of marriages, and the most equitable way to deal with the changes now so prevalent in the South. We left with new ideas, new friends, and a commitment to make this 'reunion weekend' a yearly event."

Here's an interesting aside passed along by a Tennessee woman in the music industry. "Some members of a small Baptist church in the Deep South had developed a dislike for their Yankee minister. One Sunday he announced that the Lord Jesus had presented him with the challenge of accepting the call from an out-of-state church. Shortly thereafter, the choir chimed in with the old hymnal… 'What a Friend We Have in Jesus.'"

And now, the Southern women we first introduced have a few more favorite quotes and thoughts they want to share with you. They're all the things we said they were…and more. They are fabulous friends and wonderful women, and we thank them for inspiring this book. Read on…

"Some women say they're bored; their lives have become monotonous. That's the way of nature. Look at the sun and the moon. They rise and set the same way every day. Now that's monotony. Monotony is a kind of stability that can be used to create a sense of order."   - Earth Mother

"There's a distinct difference in 'living' and being alive. We all live, but being 'alive' is the challenge."
-Wild Woman

"If we learn to appreciate what we have, we have more. If we belittle, we have less."
- Tommie

"Never put your children before your husband. Ideally, children grow up and leave but husbands stay."
- Precious

"There's only one thing we can get without sex appeal and money, and that is old age. But if we're smart, we can slow down the process with cosmetic surgery."
- Vamp

"If you aren't dealt a good hand, learn to play a poor one well."
- Wicked

"Compromise is simple once you learn to change the question to fit the answer."
- Precious

"Women will know they've made it when a man asks them for tips on how to manage a marriage and a career."
- Tommie

"If you get rejected in love or work, think of it as pruning your garden. Bigger blossoms always follow a good pruning."
- Earth Mother

"A good friend is one who stands beside you in hard times and reminds you of the lessons taught by nature. Rain is essential, but the sun always shines again."
- Earth Mother

CHAPTER 10
Fabulous Southern Food!

Food is present at every major Southern event, from reunions, weddings, funerals, family gatherings, social events, "supper clubs," picnics, and today's popular tailgating parties at such revered places as The Grove at Ole Miss. If you doubt that tailgating is a big thing down South, attend game-day at any of the 12 Southeastern Conference schools. Vanderbilt is not as high on tailgating lists because the urban campus's parking areas are limited. But if you're familiar with Nashville, you know that superb restaurants are plentiful iin Music City.

Southerners do indeed love their food, and it may be gourmet fare from Craig Claiborne's books (the late Claiborne was a native of the Mississippi Delta who became the venerable food critic for *The New York Times*) or plain old soul food of grits and greens and other down-home things.

We can't claim the late Julia Child as a Southern woman, for she hailed from the upscale side of Pasadena, California, but we can claim her attitude about food. Southerners generally enjoy good food, as did the food critic Claiborne and the late French food aficionado Julia Child. And since she has influenced many a fine Southern cook over the years, we are pleased to mention her in our book.

Even in the midst of the lettuce eaters who feared gaining an ounce, "The French Chef" (though Child referred to herself as a cook rather than a chef) aimed to satisfy the taste buds. She acknowledged the lust for red meat, sugar, eggs, real butter and good wine. She lavished attention on each step of the recipe process in order to achieve the goal, which was simply the enjoyment of excellent food.

Her long-standing advice to those who were brow-beaten with the preachings and teachings of health-food zealots: Ignore them. Ms. Child said to indulge and eat foods of all kinds, but in moderation. She advocated normal portions; never enough to feel stuffed.

As a young bride, she wanted to please her husband, a career diplomat ten years her senior and also a gourmand. She began studying French cuisine, and the rest is history. Apparently, her kitchen wisdom and wizardry worked, for Ms. Child lived a healthy 92 years and created an international reputation for herself.

Following are a few of the favorites of Southern culinary artists. I wish I could attribute all the recipes to those who created them, but they've been traded around so much, it is often impossible to attribute the origin. These recipes are tasty, not too concerned with carbs or cals, and relatively easy to prepare. They're guaranteed to enhance your reputation as a Southern cook extraordinaire! We'll follow the course of the meal, beginning with appetizers and ending with desserts. *Bon appetit!*

Photo compliments of *A Grand Heritage*. Columbus, Mississippi. Photo: the late Joe Sarcone. Home in background: Waverley Plantation, near West Point, Mississippi.

CHEESE RING WITH STRAWBERRY PRESERVES

1 lb. med. Cheddar cheese, shredded
4 green onions and tops, chopped
Mayonnaise
1/2 cup pecans, chopped
1 (8 oz.) jar strawberry preserves
Round butter crackers

Mix together softened cheese, onion, and enough mayonnaise to hold mixture together, adding one teaspoon at a time. Add nuts; shape mixture into a ring on a tray; chill. Before serving, fill center of ring with strawberry preserves and serve with round butter crackers. Good for an afternoon sherry party. Serves 12.

- A Grand Heritage

DEEP SOUTH CAVIAR

2 (15 oz.) cans black-eyed peas
1 cup vegetable oil
½ cup wine vinegar
1 clove garlic, pressed
1/2 cup onions, thinly sliced
1/2 teasp. salt
Dash of ground black pepper
Tabasco sauce to taste

Drain liquid from peas and place in a glass bowl. Add remaining ingredients and mix thoroughly. Place mixture in tightly sealed glass jar in refrigerator. Refrigerate for two or three days minimum; will keep two weeks. Serve on small party crackers. Makes about six cups.

EASY ARTICHOKE DIP

2 (14 oz.) cans artichoke hearts
1 package dry Italian dressing mix
1 cup mayonnaise

Drain artichokes; chop. Add Italian mix to mayonnaise, blend into artichokes. Serve with large corn chips. *(This is best if made day before use. Artichokes in brine are not as fat-heavy as artichokes in oil. Can also be used as a stuffing for tomatoes.)*

SMOKED OYSTER ROLL

1 (8 oz.) pkg. cream cheese
Worcestershire sauce, several dashes
Garlic salt, dash or two
1 (8 oz.) can smoked oysters
Paprika

After cream cheese has come to room temperature, mix with Worcestershire and garlic salt. Spread cream cheese mixture on rectangle of waxed paper. Cover with chopped oysters. Chill in refrigerator, then roll as a jelly roll. Sprinkle with paprika. Return to refrigerator. May be made day before.

PERFECT PIMENTO CHEESE

Mix 8 ounces of grated cheddar cheese and 3 ounces of cream cheese. Add a jar of diced pimento and stir in mayonnaise to desired consistency. Add Worcestershire sauce, onion powder, and garlic powder to taste. A pinch of sugar may be added. Use as a sandwich filler or serve with Ritz crackers as an appetizer.

-From the *Mississippi Official and Statictical Register, 1996 - 2000*

CRANBERRY SALAD

2 pkgs. Lemon Jello
1-1/4 cup hot water
1 quart cranberries
1 apple, peeled and chopped
1 orange, peeled and chopped

1 cup sugar
1/2 cup chopped pecans
3/4 cup chopped celery
1 envelope plain gelatin
Red food coloring

Mix Jello and water in large bowl. Let gel slightly; set aside. In food processor, process cranberries. Add orange and sugar; set aside. In bowl, mix celery, apple and pecans, then mix all three mixtures together. Add food coloring; chill in salad mold.

- After the Harvest

CRAB BISQUE

1 can cream of tomato soup
1 can cream of pea soup
1/2 pint coffee cream

1 can crabmeat
1 jigger of Sherry

Add all ingredients. Heat thoroughly but do not boil. Serve with chopped parsley and paprika sprinkled on top. Serves 4 to 5.

ASPARAGUS-CRAB SOUP

- 1/4 cup chopped green onion
- 1/2 teasp. curry powder
- 1 tabsp. butter
- 2 cans cream of asparagus soup
- 1 pint Half & Half
- 1/4 cup sherry
- 1 pkg. frozen crabmeat or 1 can crabmeat

Cook green onion and curry in butter; add to soup. Stir in Half & Half. Heat, but do not boil. Add sherry and crabmeat. Serves 6.

GRITS and GRILLADES

(Pronounced *gree-odds*. This is a brunch favorite in New Orleans.)

- 1 lb. round steak, cut in small pieces
- 1 large onion, chopped
- 4 tabsp. cooking oil
- 3 tabsp. flour
- 2 cups water
- Salt
- Pepper
- 1/4 teasp. thyme
- 1 tabsp. parsley
- 1/2 sm. can tomato sauce

Fry steak until brown; set aside. In the same skillet, sauté onions, add the flour and brown slightly. Add tomato sauce, water and other seasonings. Lower heat and add meat. Cover and simmer about 45 minutes. Serve with hot, cooked grits. (Some serve with rice instead of grits.)

VIDALIA ONION CASSEROLE

1/2 cup butter, divided
6 large Vidalia onions, sliced in rings
6 oz. (50) butter crackers, crushed
6 oz. shredded Parmesan cheese
Salt to taste
Paprika to taste
3 eggs, beaten
1 cup Half & Half

Preheat oven to 350. Saute onion rings in half the divided butter. Combine remaining butter with cracker crumbs. Save one-fourth cup of crumb mixture for topping; layer remaining crumbs into bottom of greased 9 x 13-inch casserole. Spread sautéed onions over crumbs and sprinkle with cheese, salt, paprika. Combine eggs and milk and pour over layers. Top with reserved crumb mixture and bake about 35 minutes.
- After the Harvest

SQUASH CASSEROLE

2 lbs. cooked squash
1 onion, sautéed in 1/2 stick butter
Salt and pepper to taste
1 cup sour cream
1/2 cup sharp cheese, grated
1/2 cup bread crumbs, buttered

Mash cooked squash and mix with other ingredients. Top with buttered bread crumbs. Bake at 350 degrees for about 15 to 20 minutes. Serves 8 to 10.

MAQUE CHOUX
(A delicious Cajun corn dish, pronounced *"mock shoe."*)

1 cup chopped onions	5 fresh tomatoes, peeled, chopped
3/4 cup bacon drippings	1/3 cup minced green pepper
12 ears fresh corn, kernels cut off	1 teaspoon salt
corn cob	1 teaspoon black pepper

Saute onions in bacon grease until transparent. Add cut-off corn and cook ten minutes, stirring constantly. Add tomatoes and green pepper and cook about five minutes or until soft. Add seasonings, including red pepper or Tabasco to taste, if desired. Serves 6.

STEWED OKRA AND TOMATOES

2 boxes frozen chopped okra	1/4 teasp. sugar
1 medium onion, chopped	Salt, garlic powder, pepper to taste
1/2 bell pepper, chopped	Red pepper or Tabasco to taste
1 can (1 lb.) stewed tomatoes	Cooking oil or bacon drippings

Saute the onion and bell pepper in a small amount of oil. When vegetables are soft, add stewed tomatoes, frozen okra, and seasonings. Cook over low heat about 30 minutes, stirring occasionally to mix okra and tomatoes. Serves 6.

FRIED GREEN TOMATOES

5 medium green tomatoes
1/3 cup flour
Salt to taste
Pepper to taste
1/2 cup shortening or oil

Select and wash firm tomatoes; cut into 1/2 inch crosswise slices. Mix flour, salt, pepper; dip both sides of tomato mixture. Fry rather quickly in sizzling oil until tomatoes are browned on the underside. Turn carefully, reduce heat, and fry until browned on other side. Remove to a platter and serve hot. Serves 4.

TOMATOES LILLIAN

4 large firm tomatoes, halved
1/2 cup butter
1/2 cup red pepper jelly
1/2 tabsp. curry powder
6 tabsp. bread crumbs

Preheat oven to 350. Arrange tomatoes in baking pan. In saucepan, heat butter, pepper jelly, curry powder. Add bread crumbs and blend. Pour jelly mixture over tomatoes. Bake until glaze is browned slightly. Serves 8.

- After the Harvest, Columbus, MS

CHOUX GLORIEUX
(Glorified cabbage, Cajun style)

1 med. head cabbage
3/4 stick butter
1 onion, chopped fine
1 can cream of mushroom soup

1/2 lb. Velveeta cheese
Bread crumbs, about 3/4 cup
Salt and red pepper to taste

Chop cabbage very fine and boil in salted water about 10 minutes. Wilt onion in butter. When wilted, add cheese in hunks and allow to melt over low heat. When cheese has melted, add mushroom soup, blending in with cheese. When blended, add cabbage and mix well. Add bread crumbs, reserving some for top of dish. Season to taste. Place in a two-quart casserole; sprinkle top with bread crumbs, bake at 350 until hot and bubbly, about 30 minutes. Serves 8.

-*Talk About Good*, Jr. League, Lafayette

FRIED OKRA

Fresh okra (tender), about 2 lbs.
Salt and pepper to taste
Corn meal

Wash and drain okra; trim tops and ends. Slice in 3/8-inch pieces. Toss okra slices in mixture of corn meal, salt and pepper. Fry in hot oil until crisp and golden brown. Drain on paper towels. Use as a vegetable side dish or as an appetizer.

MY MOTHER'S CORNBREAD DRESSING

1. Boil fat hen in salted water and onion until tender; set aside.
2. Cook corn bread (1 egg and 1/2 cup buttermilk added to 1-1/2 cup self-rising corn meal.)
3. Crumble corn bread in large container, such as a roasting pan. Add four sliceof white bread, coarsely torn.
4. Add enough chicken broth to make mixture soft.
5. Add finely-chopped onion to mixture.
6. Add five hard-boiled eggs, chopped.
7. Add 3 or 4 tablespoons of mayonnaise for added richness.
8. If mixture is still dry, add more broth; mixture must be soft.
9. Place fat hen on top and bake about one hour at 375 degrees. Keep hen moist with broth or butter

GIBLET GRAVY

Chicken liver, heart, gizzard
3/4 teasp. salt
4 tabsp. flour
3 cups giblet stock
1/8 teasp. pepper

Wash giblets (liver, heart, and gizzard); add heart, gizzard and salt to cold water and simmer 20 minutes. Add liver; cook 20 minutes longer. Drain, saving stock, chop giblets fine, add flour and brown in fat stirring constantly. Add giblet stock, stirring, and cook for five minutes. Add chopped giblets. Cream or milk may be used for part of stock. Makes three cup gravy. Serve over cornbread dressing, with cranberry sauce.

DRAMBUIE YAMS

4-6 sweet potatoes (or yams)
1/8 lb. butter
3 tabsp. honey
2 tabsp. brown sugar
2 ounces Drambuie

Steam the potatoes until tender but not soft. Let cool enough to peel. Place whole sweet potatoes in a casserole dish. Spread honey, brown sugar, butter (in chunks) and one ounce Drambuie over potatoes. Bake in moderate oven (350) for about 15 minutes. Pour remaining ounce of Drambuie over potatoes and bake for five minutes more. Cut in quarters or halves to serve. Serves 4-6.

PEAS EPICUREAN

1 can English peas
1 cup heavy cream
4 strips bacon
1/2 large while onion, chopped
1 cup mushrooms (canned or fresh)
1 tabsp. flour
Salt and pepper to taste
Dash of Worcestershire
1/4 cup Sherry

Chop uncooked bacon into pieces and sauté with onions until brown. If fresh mushrooms are used, sauté them with the onions. Add flour and cream, stirring constantly over low heat. When sauce becomes thick and smooth, add seasonings and Sherry (and canned mushrooms). Add peas and fold gently into mixture. Serves 8. *May add pimento slices for color.

CREAMED CAULIFLOWER

2 lbs. cauliflower
2 slices bread
2 cups milk
1/8 lb. butter, melted
1/2 lb. Cheddar cheese, sliced thin
1/2 cup chopped onion
1/2 cup chopped celery
Salt, black and red pepper to taste

Cut off and discard bread crust; soak remaining bread in milk for about 10 minutes. Add melted butter, onions, and celery. Season to taste and cook over medium heat until mixture forms a thick cream gravy. In separate pot, cook cauliflower (uncovered) rapidly for 20 minutes in enough boiling water to cover it. Drain well. Cut up cauliflower and cover with cream gravy. Arrange sliced cheese on top and bake at 350 degrees until cheese is melted. Serves 8.

TOMATO-CHEESE PIE

1 (9-inch) pie crust
3 ripe tomatoes, peeled
Salt and pepper to taste
1 teaspoon sweet basil
2 tabsp. chopped green onions
1 cup mayonnaise
1 cup shredded Cheddar cheese

Bake and cool crust. Fill pie crust with thick slices of ripe tomatoes. Combine remaining ingredients. Spread over tomatoes. Bake in 350 degree oven for 30 minutes; serve at once. Serves 4 to 6.

- A Grand Heritage

TOMATO ASPIC WITH ARTICHOKE HEARTS

1 (14 oz.) can whole artichoke hearts
1 (3 oz.) pkg. cream cheese
1 teasp. grated onion
1 teasp. Worcestershire sauce
Dash of Louisiana hot sauce
Salt and pepper to taste

Drain artichoke hearts well (squeeze out liquid). Combine softened cream cheese and seasonings; stuff into artichoke hearts. Put one tablespoon aspic in each individual mold. Place artichokes upside down in mold and allow to set a few minutes, then finish filling mold with aspic. Congeal.

GREEN VEGETABLE TOSS

1 (16 oz.) pkg. frozen baby limas
1 (16 oz.) pkg. frozen English peas

Cook according to package directions, or longer if softer vegetables are preferred. Drain, toss together with the following dressing. Serve hot or cold. Serves 8.

3/4 cup mayonnaise
2 boiled eggs, chopped
1/2 cup grated onion
1/2 teasp. Worcestershire
1/2 tsp. prepared mustard
Juice of 1/2 lemon
Dash garlic salt
Dash Tabasco

RICE CASSEROLE

2 tabsp. butter
4 chopped green onions
2 (4 oz.) cans cream of mushroom soup
4 cups cooked rice

1/2 cup grated Cheddar cheese
1 (6 oz.) can mushrooms
1 cup almonds, toasted, chopped

Melt butter in skillet. Saute` green onions in butter until wilted. Add soup and blend well. Mix with cooked rice in a casserole; add drained mushrooms and almonds. Top with grated cheese. Bake at 350 degrees until casserole is heated through and cheese is melted. Serves 10.

SOUTHERN FRIED CATFISH

Catfish fillets (allow 2 or 3 per person)
Buttermilk

Corn meal
Corn oil

Use thin fillets. Marinate in buttermilk for two hours. Mix cornmeal and flour (2/3 meal to 1/3 flour). Add a scant teaspoon of red pepper for every two cups of meal and flour mixture. Remove fish from buttermilk and coat with meal mixture; fry in very hot corn oil, having enough oil to cover fish. Cook in the hot oil until fish rises to the surface, at which time it is done.

MOTHER'S TURKEY CASSEROLE
(Great way to use leftover Thanksgiving turkey.)

2 cups cooked turkey	1 cup crushed potato chips
2 cups diced celery	1/2 cup toasted almonds
2 teasp. chopped green onion	1/2 teasp. salt
1 cup mayonnaise (or less; use more lemon juice)	2 tabsp. lemon juice
	1/2 cup grated sharp cheese

Preheat oven to 450. Mix all ingredients gently and place in greased casserole; bake for about ten minutes. Serves 4. *May be mixed in advance and heated before serving.

CHICKEN MARENGO

2 (2-1/2 lb.) broilers, cut up	1-1/2 cup sliced mushrooms
1/2 cup flour	2 teasp. minced parsley
1 teasp. salt	1 cup dry white wine
1 teasp. pepper	1 tabsp. brandy
1/2 cup olive oil	1 tabsp. tomato paste
4 small onions	1 tabsp. flour
1 clove garlic	

Dust cut-up chicken with seasoned flour. Heat oil and sauté chicken until golden brown. Remove and keep warm. Add one tablespoon flour to make roux. Add onions, garlic, mushrooms, parsley. Cook about five minutes, then add wine, brandy, and tomato paste. Blend all; allow to simmer about 10 minutes. Place chicken in sauce, cover, cook 30 minutes or until tender. Serve chicken and sauce over hot cooked rice. Serves 8.

- A Cook's Tour of Shreveport

SMOTHERED QUAIL

6 quail, dressed
6 tabsp. butter
3 tabsp. flour
2 cups chicken broth
1/2 cup sherry (optional)
Salt and pepper to taste
Cooked rice

Brown cleaned quail in butter in heavy skillet, then remove quail to baking dish. Add flour to butter in skillet and stir well. Slowly add chicken broth, sherry, salt and pepper. Blend well and pour over quail. Cover; bake at 350 degrees for about an hour, or until quail is tender. Serve over cooked rice, with gravy. Hot biscuits are a plus!

CRAB CAKES

4 green onions, chopped
1/3 cup mayonnaise
1 egg, beaten
1 teasp. capers
1 teasp. Cajun seasoning
1 teasp. Dijon mustard
1 lb. fresh lump crabmeat, drained
1-1/2 cup soft bread crumbs
1 tabsp. butter
1 tabsp. olive oil

Combine first six ingredients. Gently fold in crab meat and bread crumbs. Shape mixture into ten patties. Heat ½ tablespoon butter and ½ tablespoon oil in large skillet (non-stick) over medium heat. Skillet will hold about five crab cakes. Cook five patties about four minutes on each side until golden. Place on paper towels to drain; repeat procedure with remaining butter, olive oil and crab cake patties.

SHRIMP ETOUFFEE

2 lbs. fresh shrimp, peeled, deveined	4 cloves garlic, pressed
1/4 lb. butter or 3 tabsp. oil	1 tabsp. cornstarch
1 cup onions, chopped fine	1-1/2 cups water
1/2 cup celery, chopped fine	Salt, black pepper, red pepper
1/2 cup bell pepper, chopped fine	(cayenne) to taste

Split shrimp and season generously with salt, black pepper and cayenne. Set aside. Melt butter or oil and add onions, celery, bell pepper and garlic. Cook slowly in uncovered heavy pot until onions are wilted. Add seasoned shrimp and let simmer, stirring occasionally for 20 minutes. Dissolve cornstarch in water; add to mixture. Cook another 15 minutes, stirring occasionally. Serve over cooked rice. Serves 4.

OLD FASHIONED ROLLED DUMPLINGS

2-1/2 cups sifted flour	Dash pepper, or to taste
1 teasp. baking powder	1/2 cup shortening
1 teasp. salt	5 to 7 tabsp. milk

Sift flour, baking powder, salt and pepper together twice. Cut in the shortening with two knives until mixture looks like corn meal. Add milk one tablespoon at a time until it becomes a soft dough, then roll dough on a floured board to about 1/8 inch thick. Cut into inch-wide strips. Drop into cooked, boiling chicken and broth (about two quarts) and cook slowly for 15 to 20 minutes. Serves 6 to 8.

ALMOND CURRIED CHICKEN SALAD

2 teasp. curry powder
2 teasp. grated onion
1 cup mayonnaise
1/2 cup diced celery

2 cups diced chicken
1 cup diced apple
1/2 cup seedless grapes, halved
1/3 cup toasted almonds, chopped

Blend curry powder, onion, and mayonnaise. Mix with other ingredients. This can be chilled and served on lettuce leaves or toast, or stuffed in tomatoes or avacodes. Serves 4.

SHRIMP STEW

1/2 cup oil
1/4 cup flour
1 med. onion, chopped
1 cup green onions and tops
2 pods garlic, pressed
1 can tomato paste
1 tabsp. sugar

1 teasp. salt
1/2 teasp. black pepper
3 cups water
Juice of 1 lemon
1 bay leaf
Tabasco sauce to taste
2-3 lb. raw, cleaned shrimp

Brown flour in oil as in a roux. Add onions, garlic, and tomato paste, stirring until browns. Add water slowly, stirring until mixture is smooth. Add sugar, salt, pepper, bay leaf, Tabasco and lemon juice. Simmer about an hour. Add shrimp; simmer another 20 minutes. If mixture becomes too thick, add more water. Serve over hot rice.

DELTA RICE AND BLACK BEAN SALAD

- 3 cups uncooked rice
- 1 (16 oz.) can black beans, drained
- 1 med. red bell pepper, chopped
- 1 med. green bell pepper, chopped
- 4 green onions, chopped
- 1/4 cup fresh cilantro
- 1/3 cup peanut oil
- 1/4 cup lime juice
- Large lettuce leaves
- 2 avocados, peeled, sliced

In a large bowl, combine the first six ingredients. In a small bowl, whisk together oil and lime juice. Pour over rice mixture; mix lightly but well. Add salt, black and red pepper to taste. Cover and refrigerate. Serve in mounds on large lettuce leaves; garnish with avocado slices. Serves 6.

SHERRIED FRUIT

- 1 (14 oz.) can pineapple chunks
- 1 (14 oz.) can peach halves
- 1 (14 oz.) can pear halves
- 1 jar apple rings
- 1 small bottle Maraschino cherries
- 2 tabsp. flour
- 1/2 cup brown sugar, packed
- 1/2 cup butter
- 1 cup sherry

Layer drained fruits in a two quart casserole. Combine flour, brown sugar, butter, and sherry. Cook over medium heat until sugar is melted and mixture is blended. Pour sauce over layered fruit. Cover and refrigerate at least 12 hours. To serve, heat in 350 degree oven for about 20 minutes. Serves 8 to 10.

BREAD PUDDING WITH COGNAC SAUCE

2 cups milk	2 eggs, beaten
1/2 stick butter	1/8 teasp. salt
1/2 cup sugar	1/2 teasp. nutmeg
4 cups French bread cubes, day old	1 teasp. vanilla
1/2 cup raisins (optional)	1/4 cup shredded coconut (optional)

Scald milk. Melt butter in milk and stir in sugar. Pour over bread and raisins. Set stand for about 15 minutes, then add beaten eggs, salt, nutmeg, vanilla, and coconut. Bake into a greased, 1-1/2 quart dish; bake at 350 degrees for about 35 to 45 minutes. Serve warm topped with cognac sauce.

COGNAC SAUCE: 1 stick butter, 2 cups confectioners' sugar, 1/4 cup cognac. Cream butter and sugar and gradually add cognac.

OLD SOUTH PECAN PRALINES

2 cups brown sugar	1 cup water
1 cup brown sugar	1 cup cream
	3 cups pecans

Combine sugars, cream and water in a sauce pan and cook to soft ball stage (238 degrees). Remove from heat and beat until creamy. Add nuts and drop by spoonfuls onto buttered sheets.

OZARK PUDDING

- 1 egg
- 3/4 cup sugar
- 2 tabsp. flour
- 1-1/2 teaspns. baking powder
- 1/8 teasp. salt
- 1/2 cup nuts, broken
- 1 apple, diced and peeled
- 1 teasp. vanilla
- 1/2 pint whipping cream, whipped

Beat eggs and sugar until smooth. Add next three ingredients. Add nuts, apple and vanilla. Bake (350 degree pre-heated oven) in buttered 8-inch pie pan for 35 minutes. Serve with whipped cream flavor with Cointreau, or serve with ice cream or hard sauce. Serves 6-8.

RICH AND EASY CAKE

- 1 box yellow cake mix
- 1 cup sugar
- 1 (15.5 oz.) can crushed pineapple, drained

ICING

- 8 oz. cream cheese
- 1 stick softened butter or margarine
- 1 teasp. vanilla flavoring
- 1 box confectioners' sugar

Heat oven and make cake according to package directions; cook in a 9x13-inch pan. Ten minutes before cake is done, mix sugar and crushed pineapple in saucepan; boil for 5 minutes. When cake is done, punch holes in top, using a clean pencil to make holes. Pour pineapple and sugar mixture over cake. Cool. Make icing by beating together cream cheese, sugar, and vanilla. Ice cooled cake.

BLUEBERRY CREAM PIE

1 can blueberry pie filling
1 pint whipping cream
2 cups confectioners' sugar
2 teasp. vanilla
1 large pkg. cream cheese
2 baked pie shells

Whip cream and add to softened cream cheese. Combine with sugar and vanilla. Pour this mixture into two baked pie crusts. Spread one can of blueberry pie filling over the top. One can covers two 8-inch pies. Chill for several hours.

DOWN IN DIXIE BOURBON PIE

21 marshmallows
1 cup evaporated milk
1/2 pint whipping cream
3 tabsp. bourbon
Crust (see below)
Whipped cream for topping

PIE: Melt marshmallows in undiluted milk, making sure not to boil. Chill. Whip cream and fold into marshmallow mixture. Add bourbon. Pour into cooled chocolate crumb crust and refrigerate 4 hours or until set. Top with whipped cream and chocolate crumbs.

CRUST: 1 box chocolate snaps, 1/2 cup melted butter (or margarine). Crush chocolate snaps; reserve some for topping. Mix the rest with melted butter. Pat into a 9-inch pie pan and bake until set. Cool and fill with pie mixture.

Old Southern Tea Room, Vicksburg

TIPSY PUDDIN'

1 pkg. unflavored gelatin
1/4 cup cold water
2 cups milk, hot but not boiled
2 egg yolks, slightly beaten
1/2 cup sugar
1/2 cup sherry
2 egg whites, beaten 'til stiff
1 cup whipping cream, whipped
2 dozen ladyfingers, split

In bowl, soften gelatin in water. Stir in milk, egg yolks, sugar, and sherry. Chill mixture until it begins to congeal, then fold in the beaten egg whites and whipped cream. Line a 2-quart bowl with ladyfingers. Add alternate layers of the gelatin mixture and ladyfingers. Chill for a minimum of 8 hours.

AMARETTO FREEZE

1/2 gal. vanilla ice cream, softened
1 (6 oz.) carton Cool Whip
1/4 cup amaretto
Heath Bars candy, crushed

Combine ice cream with Cool Whip and amaretto. Spoon into parfait glasses; layer with crushed Heath Bars. Freeze until set. Top with more Cool Whip and additional Heath Bar crumbs. Serves 6.

- Our House Restaurant, Haley, TN.

CHOCOLATE FUDGE PIE

1/4 lb. butter
3 squares unsweetened choclate
4 eggs
3 tabsp. white Karo syrup

1-1/2 cups sugar
1/4 teasp. salt
1 teasp. vanilla
9-inch unbaked pie shell

Melt butter and chocolate together in top of double boiler. Cool slightly. Beat eggs until light then beat in syrup, sugar, salt and vanilla. Add cooled chocolate mixture and mix thoroughly. Pour into pie shell. Bake at 350 degrees for about 25 minutes, or until top is crusty and filling is set but still a little soft inside. Do not overbake. Pie should shake like custard when hot so that it will not be too stiff when cool. Serve plain or with a topping of vanilla ice cream or whipped cream.

CAFÉ BRULOT

1 stick cinnamon
6 whole cloves
Zest of med. orange, cut in slivers
Zest of med. lemon, cut in slivers

6 sugar cubes
1/2 cup brandy
2 tabsp. orange liqueur
2 cups strong black coffee

Combine cinnamon, cloves, zest, and sugar cubes in hot chafing dish; mash together with ladle. Add liqueurs, stir briefly; ignite. Continue mixing with ladle until sugar dissolves; stir in coffee gradually. When flames go out, serve in demitasse cups. What a great way to end an evening!

- A Grand Heritage

IRISH COFFEE

1 cup hot (dark roast) drip coffee
1 jigger Irish whiskey (Old Bushmill)
2 teasp. sugar
Whipped cream (canned)

Pour coffee into stemmed wine (6 ounce) glass, fill to one inch from top. Add one ounce Irish whiskey and stir in sugar. Squirt whipped cream over coffee until it stands about one inch above rim. This is a superb way to cap off a festive evening!

Road Trips That Southern Women Love!

Remember, our Southern women in this book have varied interests and backgrounds, so the road trips they chose reflect that diversity. Select what you like, and hit the road! For information on any of these places, look on the Internet, or contact the State's division of tourism or the city's convention and visitor's bureau or chamber of commerce.

* Going antiquing in small towns and remote areas across the South, looking for forgotten treasures.

* Taking the River Road down to New Orleans, checking into an old, small hotel or B&B in the French Quarter, making reservations for dinner at an outstanding restaurant, or take pot luck. Then shop, play, and dine!

* Going to literary festivals, among them the Tennessee Williams Festival in New Orleans, Clarksdale, MS, and his birthplace, Columbus, Mississippi.

* Ferreting out the best restaurants where down-home country cooking is both delicious and memorable.

* Watching a sunset or sunrise in the Florida Keys.

* Attending auctions and charity events in Palm Beach, Florida. Dress is formal, please, and wear your best jewels.

* Sitting at a sidewalk café in South Beach, drinking the drink of your choice and people watching. You'll see celebrities, but pretend you don't, because they're usually incognito.

* Discovering places like Smithville, Tennessee, where one amazing antique shop covers an entire city block, and it's one building of many!

* Finding an authentic old gristmill, now an inn near Smithville. It's a 40-acre retreat among meandering streams and rolling hills. Evins Mill is a great retreat for Southern women!

* Checking out the wineries in Middle Tennessee, among them Highland Winery and Vineyards in Jamestown, and Stonehaus Winery in Crossville. Both have gift shops and orders by the case.

* Finding old hardware and general stores in off-the-beaten-path places, such as the fabulous Cumberland General Store in Crossville, Tennessee.

* Taking a cruise on the Mississippi River, complete with exquisite food and tours of plantations along the river. A three day cruise, out of New Orleans, is a good choice.

* Finding out-of-the way art museums, as in the Lauren Rogers Museum of Art in Laurel, Mississippi. Truly one of the best small museums in the country. Spend the day there, and bring back souvenirs from the gift shop.

* Attending Broadway-type plays in an adjoining town.

- Tailgating at SEC football games.

- Finding the BEST upscale re-sale shops in the South, and among the best are in Nashville -- a superb place to play -- and Miami and Louisville, Kentucky.

- Spending a weekend at a spa and being pampered. A great one is the Grove Park Inn in Asheville, North Carolina.

- Road tripping to south Louisiana, perhaps Breaux Bridge or St. Martinville, and asking where chank-a-chank music is played. Go, learn the Cajun two-step, and then dine at Mulatte's or any other great Cajun restaurant. Some may not look like much from the outside, but the food is usually fabulous, *cher!*

- Letting the road take you to Lafayette, Louisiana, the heart of Cajun Country. A big and busy city and the one to be your base. Then, go to the outlying Cajun communities and let the good times roll! Between Lafayette and Breaux Bridge, Lake Martin offers photo opportunities galore, for it's a haven for alligators, who often sun themselves on logs in the lake.

- Spending a Christmas weekend in Natchitoches (say Nak-a-tish), Louisiana, on the Cane River. It's where "Steel Magnolias" was filmed.

- Venturing up to Shreveport, the second biggest city in Louisiana. Now a haven for gaming, with many casinos along the Red River, and Louisiana Downs for horse-racing. Great restaurants are here, and good people. Just don't lose all your money at the casinos.

* Spending a weekend in Jackson, Mississippi, going to the Jackson flea market and the Ag Museum, where you'll think you've stepped back to the past. See the Craftsmen's Guild for original art.

* Taking the Natchez Trace Parkway all the way down to Natchez, and then spending a night at an antebellum B&B, such as Monmouth or Dunleith. You'll have a taste of the real Old South. Watch the sunset over the Mississippi River from the bluff, then stroll down to Natchez Under the Hill.

* Visiting the many antique shops in Natchez. Have lunch at Stanton Hall's Carriage House Restaurant, and browse the silver shop on the same floor.

* Having a superb Sunday brunch at the historic Grand Hotel at Point Clear, Alabama.

* Attending the annual Arts and Crafts Festival in Fairhope, Alabama.

* Going to the Mountain Top Flea Market in Attalla, Alabama, where more than 1,000 booths await your perusal. Opens every Sunday at 5:00 a.m. About three miles of flea merchandise! About 60 miles n. of Birmingham.

* Planning a trip to the "First Monday" Trade Day in Ripley, Mississippi, held the first Monday of every month. Very interesting merchandise!

* Spending a Saturday night at the venerable Peabody Hotel in Memphis. Watch the ducks waddle in, then walk down Beale Street and see the sites.

* Spending a weekend at the Victorian community, Seaside, in the Florida Panhandle, and dine at near by Creola's.

* Planning a "Factory Outlet" shopping spree, where one of the best is Tanger, north of Atlanta on I-85. It's on both sides of the interstate, and a massive place!

* Going on a "treasure hunt" to such stores across the South as Hudson's and Wall's. Marshall's is much more upscale, but bargains are there, too.

* Touring the Low Country islands of South Carolina, with Beaufort or Hilton Head as your base. Fun!

* Going canoeing on the Edisto River Train in the vicinity of Charleston, South Carolina.

* Seeing the historic district of Charleston, south of Calhoun Street, where outstanding architecture and antiques abound. Great restaurants are here, too, and a must-see is the old and beautiful Trinity Episcopal Church.

* Taking advantage of Savannah, Georgia, while in this part of the South. It's a wonderful place to walk around and window shop, and an historic treasure. Great shops line the river in the old warehouse district, now River Street.

* Attending a performance at the Brevard Music Center in Brevard, North Carolina. Internationally known musicians teach and perform each summer.

* Going "leaf looking" in late October, with a prime place being the Blue Ridge Parkway in North Carolina and Virginia.

✳ Spending an exciting weekend in Atlanta, shopping at Phipps Plaza and Lenox Square, and seeing a good play or two -- perhaps at the Lyric Theater -- along with the High Museum of Art. For discount shopping, there's Loehmann's and more upscale re-sales!

✳ Finding fun and entertaining things in Louisville, Kentucky. This river city is always interesting and great to visit! Try a "hot brown" sandwich at the Brown Hotel!

✳ Attending the Spoleto Festival in Charleston, finding a Gullah woman who still uses a semblance of the dialect and weaves wonderful baskets!

✳ Visiting Columbus, Mississippi, a woman's town! See historic mansions, The "W," and reserve a stay at the Amzi Love/Lincoln Home B&B, the antebellum homes built for women.

**WHEREVER YOU GO...WHATEVER YOU DO...
REMEMBER THAT YOU'RE A FABULOUS SOUTHEN WOMAN...
SO GO AND DO IT UP IN STYLE!**

ACKNOWLEDGEMENTS

A special dedication and thanks to Beth Carden who let me stay at her perfect mountain cottage in western North Carolina so that I could finish this book. It is truly a place of the heart.

Thanks to all the Southern women who made the book possible with their wisdom, wit, common sense, and encouragement!

Thanks, especially, to good friends in Mississippi, Louisiana, Georgia, Kentucky, Florida, and North Carolina for the use of their photos throughout the book.

Thanks to the editors of *A Grand Heritage,* one of the best cookbooks in the South, for recipes and photograph. Order the cookbook from Juliaette Sharp at 662-328-3049, Columbus, Mississippi.

Thanks to my husband for his help with the business aspects of publishing this book, and thanks to our daughters, Saxonie and Shaye, for advice and input.

117

Southern belles across the South...greeting the world with graciousness.

ABOUT THE ARTIST

Artist Eugenia Talbott is a Mississippi born and bred artist who grew up on the Gulf Coast and graduated college at Mississippi University for Women. She married, had children, and stayed in Columbus until a recent re-marriage took her to the West Coast. She now lives in Medford, Oregon, though she visits her native state frequently.

Her art is seen in private collections and galleries in this country and elsewhere. She is also an interior designer, avid animal rights activist, model, and horsewoman. She is currently at work on her first book, a fictional account of a female character and her work with animal issues.

Talbott did the cover art and her photographs are seen throughout. She has two adult sons who live with their families in Mississippi, and two stepchildren. Eugenia Talbott may be contacted for commission work through Parlance Publishing: address at front and back of book.

ORDER FORM

Please send _____ copies of **SOUTHERN WOMEN** at $16.45 per copy, which includes $1.50 for shipping and handling. *Mississippi residents please include $1.15 per copy for state sales tax.* Enclosed is my check in the amount of $_____. Visa and Master card orders may be placed at 662.327.4064. Please send books to:

Name _____

Address _____

City, State _____ Zip _____

PARLANCE PUBLISHING
PO BOX 841
COLUMBUS, MS 39703-0841

Thank you